Cambridge Proficiency
Examination Practice 2

Cambridge Proficiency Examination Practice 2

University of Cambridge
Local Examinations Syndicate

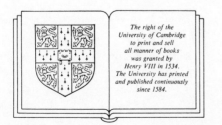

The right of the
University of Cambridge
to print and sell
all manner of books
was granted by
Henry VIII in 1534.
The University has printed
and published continuously
since 1584.

Cambridge University Press
Cambridge
New York   New Rochelle
Melbourne   Sydney

Published by the Press Syndicate of the University of Cambridge
The Pitt Building, Trumpington Street, Cambridge CB2 1RP
32 East 57th Street, New York, NY 10022, USA
10 Stamford Road, Oakleigh, Melbourne 3166, Australia

© Cambridge University Press 1987

First published 1987
Third printing 1989

Printed in Great Britain
at The Bath Press, Avon

ISBN 0 521 34910 9 Student's Book
ISBN 0 521 34911 7 Teacher's Book
ISBN 0 521 34096 9 Set of 2 cassettes

Contents

To the student   1

Practice Test 1   2

Practice Test 2   25

Practice Test 3   45

Practice Test 4   66

Practice Test 5   86

Interview Exercises   106

Acknowledgements   120

Answer Sheets   121

To the student

This book is for candidates preparing for the University of Cambridge Certificate of Proficiency in English examination and provides practice in all the written and oral papers. It contains 5 complete tests, based on the Proficiency examinations set in 1984–6, and incorporates the modifications made to Paper 5 (the Interview) in December 1985. The examination consists of 5 papers, as follows:

Paper 1 Reading Comprehension (1 hour)
   Section A consists of 25 multiple-choice items in the form of a sentence with a blank to be filled by 1 of 4 words or phrases.
   Section B consists of 15 multiple-choice items based on 2 or more reading passages of different types.

Paper 2 Composition (2 hours)
   There are 5 topics from which you choose 2. The topics include discursive, descriptive and narrative essays, a directed writing exercise and an essay based on optional reading. (In these practice tests the questions based on optional reading are set on the kind of books that are prescribed each year. These are *not* the actual books prescribed for any particular year: they are just given as examples.)

Paper 3 Use of English (2 hours)
   Section A contains exercises of various kinds which test your control of English usage and grammatical structure.
   Section B consists of a passage followed by questions which test your comprehension and skill in summarising.

Paper 4 Listening Comprehension (about 30 minutes)
   You answer a variety of questions on 3 or 4 recorded passages from English broadcasts, interviews, announcements, phone messages and conversations. Each passage is heard twice.

Paper 5 Interview (15 to 20 minutes)
   You take part in a conversation based on a photograph, passage and other material from authentic sources linked by theme, either with a group of other candidates or with the examiner alone. The exercises in these tests include some of the type set in the examination on optional reading.

Practice Test 1

PAPER 1 READING COMPREHENSION (1 hour)

Answer all questions. Indicate your choice of answer in every case **on the separate answer sheet** *already given out, which should show your name and examination index number. Follow carefully the instructions about how to record your answers. Give* **one answer only** *to each question. Marks will not be deducted for wrong answers: your total score on this test will be the number of correct answers you give.*

SECTION A

In this section you must choose the word or phrase which best completes each sentence. **On your answer sheet** *indicate the letter A, B, C or D against the number of each item 1 to 25 for the word or phrase you choose.*

1 When he woke up, he realised that the things he had dreamt about could not
.... have happened.
   A possibly   B likely   C certainly   D potentially

2 £50? £70? Let's .... the difference and say £60.
   A avoid   B split   C agree   D decrease

3 The leaders, sensing that war was ...., prepared their defences.
   A immediate   B immune   C immense   D imminent

4 There is a lot of friendly .... between the supporters of the two teams.
   A contest   B rivalry   C contention   D defiance

5 He read it through quickly so as to get the .... of it before settling down to a thorough study.
   A detail   B run   C core   D gist

6 The purpose of the survey was to .... the inspectors with local conditions.
   A inform   B acquaint   C instruct   D notify

7 My wife's being .... for migraine headaches at the clinic.
   A cured   B healed   C operated   D treated

8 Despite the high divorce rate, the .... of marriage remains popular.
   A practice   B habit   C institution   D state

9   He drove fast and arrived an hour .... of schedule.
    A in advance   B ahead   C abreast   D in front

10 I'd like to .... this old car for a new model but I can't afford it.
    A interchange   B exchange   C replace   D convert

11 They were awaiting official .... of the news they had heard from a friend.
    A recommendation   B statement   C confirmation   D announcement

12 Although they usually did their own painting and papering, on this occasion they
    brought in a firm of .... decorators.
    A inside   B inward   C interior   D internal

13 In my opinion standards of workmanship have .... over the past twenty
    years.
    A aggravated   B diminished   C deteriorated   D eroded

14 He tries to .... himself with everyone by paying them compliments.
    A gratify   B please   C ingratiate   D commend

15 When the police examined the house they found that the lock had been ....
    with.
    A touched   B tampered   C broken   D hindered

16 In those days a girl could not get married if her father .... his consent.
    A forbade   B upheld   C rejected   D withheld

17 The zoo attendant opened the cage and tried to .... the animal back in.
    A coax   B induce   C seduce   D convince

18 The ruling party is worried in case they lose .... control of the City Council
    in the forthcoming elections.
    A overall   B whole   C unanimous   D mass

19 I liked the coat but was rather .... off by the price.
    A shaken   B put   C set   D held

20 This man is so arrogant that he is completely .... to all criticism.
    A impervious   B unaware   C regardless   D unconscious

21 The accusation left him quite .... with rage.
    A dumb   B silent   C speechless   D mute

22 The local medical officer reported a serious .... of food-poisoning.
    A state   B incident   C outbreak   D event

⟫→

[3]

23 No matter how angry he was he would never .... to violence.
   A resolve   B recourse   C exert   D resort

24 He was so .... in the TV programme that he forgot to turn the oven off.
   A distracted   B attracted   C gripped   D engrossed

25 The man was very conscious .... his bald head.
   A about   B with   C of   D for

SECTION B

In this section you will find after each of the passages a number of questions or unfinished statements about the passage, each with four suggested answers or ways of finishing. You must choose the one which you think fits best according to the passage. **On your answer sheet**, *indicate the letter A, B, C or D against the number of each item 26 to 40 for the answer you choose. Give* **one answer only** *to each question. Read each passage right through before choosing your answers.*

FIRST PASSAGE

It being not only possible but even easy to predict which ten-year-old boys are at greatest risk of growing up to be persistent offenders, what are we doing with the information? Just about the last thing that we should do is to wait until their troubles have escalated in adolescence and then attack them with the provisions of the new Criminal Justice Bill.

If this bill becomes law, magistrates will have the power to impose residential care orders. More young people will be drawn into institutional life when all the evidence shows that this worsens rather than improves their prospects. The introduction of short sharp shocks in detention centres will simply give more young people a taste of something else they don't need; the whole regime of detention centres is one of toughening delinquents, and if you want to train someone to be anti-establishment, "I can't think of a better way to do it," says the writer of this report.

The Cambridge Institute of Criminology comes up with five key factors that are likely to make for delinquency: a low-income family, a large family, parents deemed by social workers to be bad at raising children, parents who themselves have a criminal record, and low intelligence in the child. Not surprisingly, the factors tend to overlap. Of the 63 boys in the sample who had at least three of them when they were ten, half became juvenile delinquents – compared with only a fifth of the sample as a whole.

Three more factors make the prediction more accurate: being judged troublesome by teachers at the age of ten, having a father with at least two criminal convictions and having another member of the family with a criminal record. Of the 35 men who had at least two of these factors in their background, 18 became persistent delinquents and 8 more were in trouble with the law.

Among those key factors, far and away the most important was having a parent with a criminal record, even if that had been acquired in the distant past, even though very few parents did other than condemn delinquent behaviour in their children.

The role of the schools emerges as extremely important. The most reliable prediction of all on the futures of boys came from teachers' ratings of how troublesome they were at the age of ten. If the information is there in the classroom there must be a response that brings more attention to those troublesome children: a search for things to give them credit for other than academic achievement, a refusal to allow them to go on playing truant, and a fostering of ambition and opportunity which should start early in their school careers.

26 According to the author, delinquency should be dealt with
   A   before adolescence.
   B   during institutional treatment.
   C   during adolescence.
   D   when the problem becomes acute.

27 The number of young offenders could be reduced by
   A   new legal measures.
   B   better residential care.
   C   brief periods of harsh punishment.
   D   examination of their backgrounds.

28 What is the result of putting young offenders into detention centres?
   A   They become more violent.
   B   They receive useful training.
   C   They become used to institutions.
   D   They turn against society.

29 Ten-year-old children likely to become offenders are often
   A   spoilt children from small families.
   B   bright children in a poor family.
   C   dull children with many brothers and sisters.
   D   children whose parents have acquired wealth dishonestly.

30 Most parents of young offenders
   A   deny that their child is a delinquent.
   B   blame their own criminal activities.
   C   disapprove of their child's behaviour.
   D   blame the school for the child's behaviour.

31 The writer concludes that potential offenders could be helped by
   A   spending more time at school.
   B   more encouragement at school.
   C   more activities outside school.
   D   stricter treatment from teachers.

SECOND PASSAGE

"Here we are!" William flung open the door of his office and we went in. Two elderly grey men were sitting at a table, one with a bag of sweets which he hastily put away into a drawer, the other with a card-index which he naturally did not attempt to conceal. William did not acknowledge them in any way nor did they take any notice of him. He sat down at an enormous desk in the centre of the room, which had two telephones on it and a line of wire baskets, importantly labelled and stacked with files.

"This is a nice room," I said, going to the window, "and what a lovely desk you have." I felt embarrassed at the presence of the grey men and did not quite know what to say. But suddenly a rattling sound, as if a trolley was being wheeled along the corridor, was heard and the two men leaped up, each carrying a china mug.

"Oh, excuse me," said William, leaping up too and taking a china mug from a drawer in his desk, "I think I hear the tea."

He did not offer to get me any, nor did I feel I really wanted any as it was barely three o'clock. I wondered why the grey men, who were obviously of a lower status than William, had not fetched his tea for him, but perhaps there was a rigid etiquette in these matters. Also, knowing William's fussiness, it was quite likely that he would insist on fetching his own tea.

I went on standing by the window and looked out at the view, which was of another office building, perhaps the same Ministry. Grey men sat at desks, their hands moving among files; some sipped tea, one read a newspaper, another manipulated a typewriter with the uncertain touch of two fingers. A girl leaned from a window, another combed her hair, a third typed with expert speed. A young man embraced a girl in a rough playful way and she pulled his hair while the other occupants of the room looked on encouragingly ... I watched, fascinated, and was deep in contemplation when William and his underlings came back with their steaming mugs.

32   What word best describes the behaviour of the man with the sweets?
    A   guilty
    B   efficient
    C   mean
    D   childish

33   The narrator commented on William's desk because she
    A   was impressed by its size.
    B   felt she had to say something.
    C   wanted to see his files.
    D   wanted to make the grey men talk.

34   The narrator supposed that William fetched his own tea because
    A   the grey men disliked him.
    B   he wanted to leave the office for a moment.
    C   he wanted his tea to be just right.
    D   each man had his own mug.

35 The narrator is fascinated by the other office block because
    A   the people there are not working properly.
    B   so many activities are going on there.
    C   the people seem much friendlier than in William's office.
    D   she wonders what kind of work they are doing.

THIRD PASSAGE

For the past 20 years London's public transport system has been in decline. The fall in passengers has pushed up the fares to drive away even more people. And the result has been more and more cars on increasingly congested roads and a public transport system starved of cash.

Help decide London Transport's future NOW!

What happens to London Transport will affect the lives of everyone in London for years to come. That is why the Greater London Council believes that you, the people of London, should have a say in the future. We have drawn up four different options to present to the Secretary of State for Transport. But we also want to be able to tell him what YOU think about them.

APPROACH A "Break Even"

If London Transport were to be run as a commercial business then by 1987:

- bus services would be cut by 40%;
- bus and underground fares would rise by 40% on top of inflation;
- tube services would be cut by 3% and up to 20 stations and five sections of line would disappear;
- less use of public transport would mean the direct loss of 12,000 jobs;
- there would be even more traffic congestion and more accidents.

APPROACH B "Cash Limits"

(What we have now)
Working on the basis of current Government policy:

- today's fares would rise in line with inflation;
- bus services would be cut by 16%;
- underground services would be cut by 3% and up to 10 stations would be closed; some 5,000 jobs would be lost;
- traffic congestion and accidents would increase by about half that of the "Break Even" approach.

APPROACH C "Minimum Needs"

If, after a change in the law, the Government gave London Transport a direct level of subsidy comparable with even minor urban transport systems in Europe:

- fares would be restored to their pre-March 1982 levels – the Fares Fair scheme – but would rise with inflation;
- bus services would be cut by 5% and tube services would increase by 6%;
- four or five stations would close;
- increased use of buses and tube would lead to a 3% reduction in road traffic congestion, and fewer road accidents.

APPROACH D "Fares Fair"

With Government support raised, by a change in the law, to the level of most major urban transport systems in other countries:

- fares would be halved and then frozen;
- by 1987 fares would be 65% lower than today after inflation was taken into account;
- bus services would improve by 13% and the underground by the maximum 6% possible; London's traffic problems would be eased considerably.

36 Which approach does the Greater London Council believe to be the most harmful for the people of London?
    A   B   C   D

37 Which approach does the Greater London Council favour most?
    A   B   C   D

38 Which approach would probably result in the most accidents?
    A   B   C   D

39 Which scheme depends on the Government giving as much money to London Transport as other Governments give to transport in big cities?
    A   B   C   D

40 The aim of this advertisement is to
    A   persuade you to use London Transport more.
    B   report on the state of London Transport today.
    C   convince you that London Transport needs a subsidy.
    D   publicise the faults of London Transport.

PAPER 2   COMPOSITION   (2 hours)

*Write **two only** of the following composition exercises. Your answers must follow exactly the instructions given. Write in pen, not pencil. You are allowed to make alterations, but see that your work is clear and easy to read.*

1   Imagine you are a nurse in a busy hospital. Write a descriptive account of a working day. (About 350 words)

2   "Large-scale unemployment, with all its problems, is now a permanent feature of our society." Discuss. (About 350 words)

3   Write a story which ends as follows: "He picked up the unopened envelope and set light to it with a match. With a faint smile on his face, he watched the remains crumble in the ashtray." (About 350 words)

4

Adventure holidays in Scotland

A leading holiday company requires group leaders to supervise children aged 12-18 years. Applicants must be capable of organising a wide range of social and outdoor activities. Ability to give instructions in one of the following: scuba diving, mountain climbing, horse-riding, or any other suitable speciality will be an advantage. Long hours of demanding work are necessary, but a good salary will be paid to the right person.

Applications with full details to:

Jim McKinlay,

Camp Scotland, 14 Theatre St, Glasgow.

Write a letter in reply to the above newspaper advertisement. (About 300 words)

5   Basing your answer on your reading of the prescribed text concerned, answer *one* of the following. (About 350 words)

SHAKESPEARE: *Macbeth*
What is the significance of the Witches in the play?

SCOTT FITZGERALD: *The Great Gatsby*
Everyone went to Gatsby's parties; no-one attended his funeral. How do you account for this?

ARNOLD WESKER: *Roots*
Describe the kind of life the Bryant family lived and explain what Beatie thought was wrong with it.

PAPER 3   USE OF ENGLISH   (2 hours)

SECTION A

1   *Fill each of the numbered blanks in the following passage with* **one** *suitable word.*

How would you write today's date in figures? Current practice varies considerably and a "great debate" is now in .... (1) to establish ....*the*............. (2) universally acceptable method. In Britain ....*we*........... (3) usually puts the day ....*first*.............. (4), followed by the month and then the year, ...*but*........... (5) in America it's the other way ......*down ?*............ (6), so that the nineteenth of June 1984 would be written 6-19-84. .... (7) such variations can ....*put*........... (8) confusion in the computerised international world of industry, businessmen are now pressing .... (9) a uniform procedure for the numerical writing of dates.

The problem is: ......*which*......... (10) country's method ....*with*............ (11) be adopted? Britain's, America's or something dreamed ....*of*........... (12) by a committee? Understandably, ...*no*.............. (13) country is all .... (14) keen to give up its .....*own*........... (15) tradition and adopt somebody else's. The French International Organisation for Standardisation has come up with a possible solution. It proposes that ....*the*.......... (16) numerically written dates should appear in descending

[12]

...*was*... (17) with the year first, then the month and ...*finally*....

(18) the day. The drawback here is that .... (19) any countries

seem in favour of this idea and the majority are most ...*likely*...... (20) to

implement it.

2 *Finish each of the following sentences in such a way that it means exactly the same as the sentence printed before it.*

   EXAMPLE: I expect that he will get there by lunchtime.

   ANSWER: I expect him *to get there by lunchtime*.

   a) "Let's go for a walk in the park," said Andrew.

       Andrew suggested that ...*we should go for a walk in the park*

   b) His second attempt on the world record was successful.

       He broke ...*the world record at his second attempt*

   c) Helen can play the piano better than Elizabeth.

       Elizabeth ...*can't play the piano as well as Helen can*

   d) I'm sure he didn't know that his brother was seriously ill.

       He couldn't possibly ...*know about his brother's serious illness*

   e) What particularly impressed me was her excellent command of English.

       I ...*was particularly impressed by her excellent*...

   f) She didn't say a word as she left the room.

       She left the room ...*without saying a word*

   g) The result of the match was never in doubt.

       At no time ...*there was we doubt about the result of*...

   h) This will be the orchestra's first performance outside London.

       This will be the first time ...*the orchestra play outside London*

[13]

3 *Fill each of the blanks with a suitable word or phrase.*

> EXAMPLE: Even if I had stood on a chair, *I wouldn't have been able to* reach the light bulb.

a) Give ~~me a ring~~ tomorrow evening. My number is 367 2215.

b) What time do you call this? We ~~have been waiting~~ for you for nearly half an hour!

c) My sister wasn't in Paris last month so you ~~can't have~~ seen her there.

d) The occupant of the burning flat was taken to hospital ~~in a state of~~ shock.

e) ~~if you don't bring back~~ those books to the library immediately, you will have to pay a fine.

f) He deserves the maximum penalty ~~for~~ a crime.

4 *For each of the sentences below, write a new sentence* **as similar as possible in meaning to the original sentence,** *but using the word given. This word must* **not** *be altered in any way.*

> EXAMPLE: John inflated the tyres of his bicycle.
> **blew**

> ANSWER: *John blew up the tyres of his bicycle.*

a) I'd rather we started at seven.
   preference
   ~~My preference is that we would start at seven~~

b) There'll be trouble if you do that again.
   better
   ~~you would better~~

c) The accident wasn't his fault.
   blame
   ~~he wasn't to blame for the accident~~

d) Most people know that Britain's economy is heavily dependent on North Sea oil.
   common

   ....

e) I'd be grateful if you would check these accounts for me.
   mind

   Do you mind checking the accounts for me?

f) It's unlikely that the contractor will complete the work before February.
   take

   it will take more time to the contractor

g) That jumper you knitted for my daughter no longer fits her.
   grown

   My daughter has grown up so much

SECTION B

5   *Read the following passage, then answer the questions which follow it.*

Imagine that someone is being shown a pair of cards. On one of them there is a line, and on the other, three lines. Of these three, one is obviously longer than the line on the first card, one is shorter, and one is the same length. The person to whom these cards are being shown is asked to point to the line on the second card which is the same length as the line on the first card.   5
Surprisingly, the person concerned makes one of the obviously wrong choices. You might suppose that he (or she) perhaps suffers from distorted vision or is insane. But you could be wrong: you might be observing a sane, ordinary citizen just like yourself. By fairly simple processes, sane and ordinary citizens can be induced to deny the plain evidence of their senses –   10
not always, but often. In recent years psychologists have carried out some interesting experiments illustrating the methods by which this can be achieved.
    The general procedure is as follows: someone is asked to join a group of people who are helping to study the perception of length. The victim, having   15
agreed to this seemingly innocent request, goes to a room where about half a dozen other participants and the experimenter are seated. Unknown to the victim, none of the other people in the room is a volunteer like himself; they are all in league with the experimenter. A pair of cards like those described above is produced, and each participant in turn is asked to state which of the   20
three lines on the second card is equal in length to the line on the first card.

[15]

Without hesitation, they all pick the same, wrong line because they have previously been primed to do so by the experimenter. The latter also ensures that the turn of the volunteer comes last of all. In many cases, faced with this unanimity, the volunteer denies the obvious facts of the case and agrees.   25

In another experiment sounds were used instead of lines, and the subjects were merely asked to determine which of two successive sounds was of longer duration. The volunteer would come into a room where there was a row of five cubicles with their doors shut, and one open cubicle for him. He would sit in it and put on the earphones provided. He would then hear the   30
occupants of the other cubicles tested in turn, and each would give the wrong answer. But the other cubicles were, in fact, unoccupied, and what he heard were tape-recordings played by the experimenter. A team of research workers conducted a series of tests using this technique in which they varied the pressure exercised on the subjects and demonstrated conclusively that,   35
faced with the unanimous opinion of the group they were in, people could be made to deny the plain evidence of their senses in up to 75 per cent of the trials. You may reply that there is no cause for alarm because in real situations the total unanimity of a group is rare. Nevertheless, I find this more than a trifle alarming.   40

a) What were the "wrong choices" mentioned in lines 6 and 7?

....

....

b) What is meant by the phrase "suffers from distorted vision" (lines 7 and 8)?

....

c) What is meant by the phrase "seemingly innocent" (line 16)?

....

d) Give an alternative expression for "in league with" (line 19).

....

e) What does the volunteer in fact do when his turn comes?

....

....

f) Why does the experimenter make sure that the volunteer is the last person to answer?

....

....

g) Explain the phrase "two successive sounds" (line 27).

....

h) Why did some of the cubicles have their doors shut?

....

....

i) What was the experimenter doing while the volunteer was sitting in his cubicle?

....

j) What special meaning has the word "subjects" in this passage?

....

k) What is meant by "the total unanimity of a group" (line 39)?

....

....

l) What is it that the author finds "more than a trifle alarming" (lines 39 and 40)?

....

....

m) In a paragraph of 80–100 words summarise the experimental techniques used to persuade people to conform to the opinion of the group.

....

⋙→

....

....

....

....

....

....

....

PAPER 4   LISTENING COMPREHENSION
(about 30 minutes)

FIRST PART

For questions 1–6, fill in the correct answer.

Item purchased	1	HOUSE
Price	2	38 000£
Repairs	3	ROOF
and	4	REWIRING
Renovation	5	Painting
Month of taking possession	6	APRIL

For questions 7–11, put a tick in one of the boxes A, B, C or D.

7   What is the relationship between the speaker and the caller?

A ✗	friend/friend
B	builder/client
C	fiancé/fiancée
D	lawyer/client

8   The speaker thinks the caller has

A ✗	got a bargain.
B	made a profit.
C	paid the asking price.
D	paid too much.

9   Why does the speaker offer to help?

A	He has useful business contacts.
B	He can get material cheaply.
C ✗	He has previous experience.
D	It's his job.

10   Why did the caller ring?

A	to ask for money
B	to ask for help
C ✗	to give some news
D	to arrange a meeting

11   How soon do they plan to meet?

A ✗	that evening
B	the following morning
C	the following evening
D	later in the week

SECOND PART

For each of questions 12–17 tick one of the pictures A, B, C or D in the boxes provided.

12   Which of these is used in making the hand exerciser?

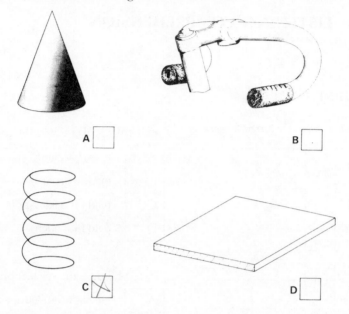

A ☐   B ☐

C ☒   D ☐

13   Which of these is used to measure how strong your fingers are?

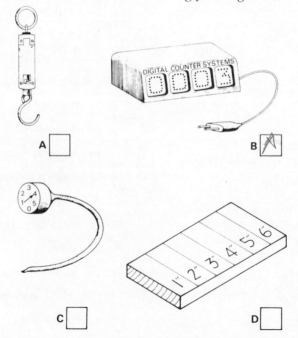

A ☐   B ☒

C ☐   D ☐

14   Which parts of the body does *Physiotherapy Aids* deal with?

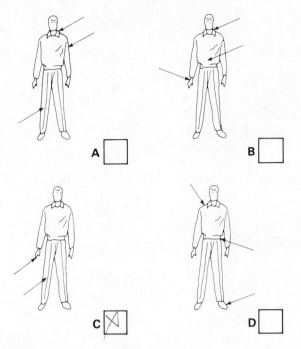

A ☐   B ☐

C ☒   D ☐

15   Which one of these is used for the leg exerciser?

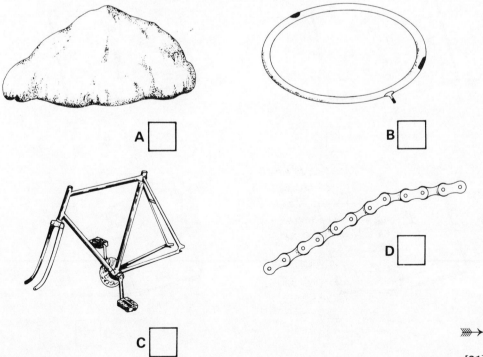

A ☐   B ☐

C ☐   D ☐

⟫→

16 How is the rubber arranged for an adult's and a child's exerciser?

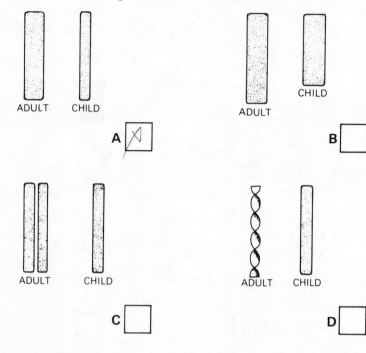

A

B

C

D

17 What does *Physiotherapy Aids* look like?

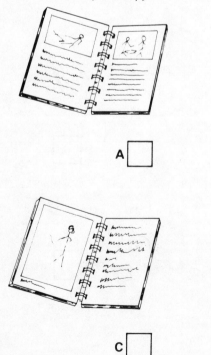

A

B

C

D

THIRD PART

Fill in the gaps numbered 18–25 in the advertisement below. Some have been filled in for you.

GREAT HOLIDAY BARGAINS!!

PRICES SLASHED!!

Try Delta's special Money-saving

(18) .... *offers* .... and save up to (19) .... *35 £* ....

on a holiday in GREECE!

Spend a (20) .... *fortnight* .... on the beautiful

island of Corfu for just £140!

Accommodation in a (21) .... *villa* .... or taverna.

Camping holidays in (22) .... *France* .... Greenfields

offer big savings on (23) .... *family* .... holidays

if you go before 25th (24) .. *of june* ....

(25) .... *12* .... nights camping will cost

your family of four just £160!

FOR MORE DETAILS CONTACT YOUR TRAVEL AGENT *NOW!*

PAPER 5   INTERVIEW   (15–20 minutes)

You will be asked to take part in a conversation with a group of other students or with your teacher. The conversation will be based on one particular topic area or theme, for example holidays, work, food.

Of course each interview will be different for each student or group of students, but a *typical* interview is described below.

★ At the start of the interview you will be asked to talk about one of the photographs among the Interview Exercises at the back of the book.

★ You will then be asked to discuss one of the passages at the back of the book. Your teacher may ask you to talk about its content, where you think it comes from, who the author or speaker is, whether you agree or disagree with it, and so on. You will *not* be asked to read the passage aloud, but you may quote parts of it to make your point.

★ You may then be asked to discuss for example an advertisement, a leaflet, extract from a newspaper etc. Your teacher will tell you which of the Interview Exercises to look at.

★ You may also be asked to take part in an activity with a group of other students or your teacher. Your teacher will tell you which section among the Interview Exercises you should look at.

Practice Test 2

PAPER 1 READING COMPREHENSION   (1 hour)

Answer all questions. Indicate your choice of answer in every case **on the separate answer sheet** *already given out, which should show your name and examination index number. Follow carefully the instructions about how to record your answers. Give* **one answer only** *to each question. Marks will not be deducted for wrong answers: your total score on this test will be the number of correct answers you give.*

SECTION A

In this section you must choose the word or phrase which best completes each sentence. **On your answer sheet** *indicate the letter A, B, C or D against the number of each item 1 to 25 for the word or phrase you choose.*

1   He cannot .... ignorance as his excuse; he should have known what was happening in his own department.
    A insist   B plead   C refer   D defend

2   Visitors are .... to beware of pickpockets.
    A commanded   B informed   C notified   D advised

3   If you don't pay your bill, the Electricity Board will .... your power supply.
    A dismantle   B sever   C disconnect   D uncouple

4   He did not share his secrets with many people but he .... in her.
    A confessed   B concealed   C consented   D confided

5   Before you can start a business, you will have to raise the necessary ....
    A investment   B income   C savings   D capital

6   As the drug took .... the patient became quieter.
    A force   B influence   C action   D effect

7   She was a devoted nurse, always very .... to the needs of her elderly patients.
    A attentive   B observant   C earnest   D careful

8   They .... great difficulty saving up enough money for a house.
    A found   B incurred   C had   D achieved

9   The mountaineers had to .... severe cold and high winds.
     A outlive   B attain   C go through   D endure

10   After three weeks off work, David found that time was beginning to ....
     A relax   B drag   C delay   D extend

11   He has been offered the job .... to his passing a medical examination.
     A confirmatory   B provisional   C subject   D dependent

12   I was completely .... by most of the exam questions, so I must have failed.
     A stupified   B baffled   C stultified   D harrassed

13   The unpleasant smell in the restaurant .... me off my dinner.
     A set   B put   C sent   D took

14   If he loses consciousness, give him a sip of brandy to bring him ....
     A up   B back   C round   D over

15   They .... on the secret passage while they were exploring the caves.
     A stumbled   B foundered   C fumbled   D tripped

16   Please .... from smoking until the plane is airborne.
     A refrain   B exclude   C resist   D restrain

17   He was a generous friend but as a businessman he drove a hard ....
     A bargain   B affair   C contract   D deal

18   The unscrupulous salesman .... the old couple out of their life savings.
     A deprived   B swindled   C robbed   D extracted

19   The civil rights movement was in its .... in the 1960s.
     A top   B heyday   C summit   D pitch

20   Has he changed his mind again? I wish he'd at least be ....
     A constant   B congenial   C compatible   D consistent

21   A prime minister cannot expect to have much time to .... to purely personal matters.
     A reserve   B devote   C concentrate   D spare

22   We have .... into your claim of wrongful dismissal but can find nothing to support it.
     A probed   B looked   C examined   D investigated

23   Your argument .... that Britain is still a great power, but this is no longer
      the case.
      A outlines   B presupposes   C concerns   D presents

24   It was surprising that he showed so little .... at his sister's death.
      A feelings   B sympathy   C grief   D involvement

25   The situation was .... complicated by John's indecision.
      A more   B extra   C further   D altogether

SECTION B

*In this section you will find after each of the passages a number of questions or unfinished
statements about the passage, each with four suggested answers or ways of finishing. You must
choose the one which you think fits best according to the passage.* **On your answer sheet**,
*indicate the letter A, B, C or D against the number of each item 26 to 40 for the answer you
choose. Give* **one answer only** *to each question. Read each passage right through before
choosing your answers.*

FIRST PASSAGE

The ownership of pets brings a variety of benefits that the uninitiated would never
believe. For every tale of shredded cushions, flattened plants and chewed slippers, there
is another testimonial of intelligence, sympathy and undying devotion. Now the
growing body of research into the medical and social advantages of pet ownership has
confirmed what pet owners have always intuitively known: that pets are not just loving
companions but actually do us good. Researchers have established the value of pets in
soothing and reassuring humans, particularly when ill, lonely or in distress. Perhaps the
unquestioning love and approval pets give us is something we don't always get from
our human nearest and dearest.
      Our makeshift understanding of psychology leads many of us to view very close
relationships with pets with suspicion. Childless couples in particular give rise to
speculation, but a consultant in animal behaviour says, "There is no evidence that a pet
is a direct substitute for a child." And while many adults feel foolish if caught talking to
their pets, they have no need to. The experts say you cannot have a close relationship
with a pet without treating it as a person and that talking to a pet is not unhealthy –
simply a way of establishing rapport.
      The wobbling helplessness of a young puppy or a fluffy kitten stirs protective
instincts deep within us and prompts many parents to buy pets for their children in the
hope of instilling a sense of responsibility and caring and acceptance of the facts of life
and death. But animals don't have to be soft and cuddly to bring out the best in us. A
social worker encouraged aggressive boys to handle ferrets – "If handled correctly they
respond with friendship; if incorrectly they bite."
      There seems to be no doubt that, emotionally and physically, our pets do us good
– but there is a price to be paid. When a loved animal dies it is often a traumatic event –
and then where do we turn for comfort?

26 Pets are sometimes criticised because they
   A   lack intelligence.
   B   need considerable care.
   C   are destructive.
   D   demand affection.

27 The idea that animals are a substitute for children is
   A   supported by research.
   B   encouraged by psychologists.
   C   an argument for keeping a pet.
   D   a common prejudice.

28 Talking to animals is
   A   silly.
   B   beneficial.
   C   suspicious.
   D   stimulating.

29 When choosing a pet you should remember that
   A   a young animal is best for everyone.
   B   the animal need not be attractive.
   C   certain animals can be dangerous.
   D   a ferret makes a good pet.

30 The writer believes that pets are valuable to children because they
   A   return affection.
   B   need looking after.
   C   are comforting.
   D   are protective.

SECOND PASSAGE

Until recently, women in advertisements wore one of three things—an apron, a glamorous dress or a frown. Although that is now changing, many women still feel angry enough to deface offending advertisements with stickers protesting, "This ad degrades women". Why does this sort of advertising exist? How can advertisers and ad agencies produce, sometimes after months of research, advertising that offends the consumer?

The Advertising Standards Authority (the body which deals with complaints about print media) is carrying out research into how women feel about the way they are portrayed in advertisements. Its conclusions are likely to be what the advertising industry already knows: although women are often irritated by the way they are seen in ads, few feel strongly enough to complain.

Women are not the only victims of poor and boring stereotypes – in many TV commercials men are seen either as useless, childish oafs who are unable to perform the simplest household tasks, or as inconsiderate boors, permanently on the lookout for an escape to the pub. But it is women who seem to bear the brunt of the industry's apparent inability to put people into an authentic present-day context.

Yet according to Emma Bennett, executive creative director of a London advertising agency, women are not infuriated by stereotypes and sexist advertising. "It tends to wash over them; they are not militant or angry – they just find it annoying or tiresome. They reluctantly accept outdated stereotypes, but heave a sigh of relief when an advertisement really gets it right."

She says that it is not advertising's use of the housewife role that bothers women, but the way in which it is handled. "Researchers have often asked the wrong questions. The most important thing is the advertisement's tone of voice. Women hate being patronised, flattered or given desperately down-to-earth commonsense advice."

In the end, the responsibility for good advertising must be shared between the advertiser, the advertising agency and the consumer. Advertising does not set trends but it reflects them. It is up to the consumer to tell advertisers where they fail, and until people on the receiving end take the business seriously and make their feelings known, the process of change will remain laboriously slow.

31 Despite recent changes in attitudes, some advertisements still fail to
   A change women's opinions of themselves.
   B show any understanding of people's feelings.
   C persuade the public to buy certain products.
   D meet the needs of the advertising industry.

32 According to the writer, the commonest fault of present-day advertising is to
   A condemn the role of the housewife.
   B ignore protests about advertisements.
   C present a misleading image of women.
   D misrepresent the activities of men.

33 Research suggests that the reaction of women towards misrepresentation by advertisements is
   A apathy.
   B hostility.
   C approval.
   D relief.

34 Emma Bennett suggests that advertisements should
   A give further emphasis to practical advice.
   B change their style rather than their content.
   C use male images instead of female ones.
   D pay more compliments to women than before.

35 Ultimately the advertising industry should
   A take its job more seriously.
   B do more pioneering work.
   C take notice of public opinion.
   D concentrate on the products advertised.

THIRD PASSAGE

A

Pisces
*February 20
to March 20*

This month you come face to face with a number of purely practical issues involving property, possessions and partnerships. Begin with some heart-searching: can you afford to continue as you are? Are you living beyond your means? How much security are you guaranteed in your present job? Are you being given the scope you deserve? No matter how much you are enjoying your work, you probably feel that you need more freedom to display your talents. If so, this is a perfect time to put forward your case and ask for promotion. Sadly, money matters look a lot less straightforward.

B

Leo
*July 21
to August 21*

Mars continuing to cross your sign restores confidence, renews ambition and raises your hopes. So whatever happens – and quite a lot will – you will have the strength and optimism to stay on top. But it is vitally important that you channel your new-found drive in the right direction. You may have to sacrifice your social life – at least for a while – in order to concentrate on other things. You will be forced to face up to your responsibilities, both personal (involving family, relatives and friends) and financial (in the form of joint commitments, overdrafts, loans etc.), and you can no longer afford to ignore the boring paperwork.

C

Libra
*September 23
to October 22*

October should prove a boom month. Be brave. Be bold. Be daring. Don't hesitate to take on extra work – even if you feel you won't be able to cope (you will!). Seize any opportunity which may further your career (there will be plenty). You should be ready to work **and** play hard. There will be exciting developments on the social front, bringing new people into your life and giving you every chance to extend your circle. Even business trips look surprisingly enjoyable.

D

Capricorn
*December 21
to January 19*

It is quite clear that the most pressing factor in your life at the moment is your career. There are two main points to consider: first, be sure to give colleagues and employees the incentives and encouragement they deserve, and second, try to prepare yourself for a number of minor difficulties which could easily sap your confidence and play on your nerves. There will probably be some moments of despondency and self-doubt and you will have to fight hard to ward them off.

36 Which of these horoscopes suggests that a more serious approach to life is needed?
   A   B   C   D

37 Which horoscope suggests that some people feel limited in their work?
   A   B   C   D

38 Which horoscope advises against being cautious?
   A   B   C   D

39 Which horoscopes predict the least promising future?
   A   Pisces and Leo
   B   Leo and Capricorn
   C   Libra and Leo
   D   Pisces and Capricorn

40 From their content, we can deduce that these horoscopes come from a magazine bought by
   A   young people.
   B   business people.
   C   married people.
   D   well-off people.

PAPER 2   COMPOSITION   (2 hours)

*Write **two only** of the following composition exercises. Your answers must follow exactly the instructions given. Write in pen, not pencil. You are allowed to make alterations, but see that your work is clear and easy to read.*

1   Suggest some ways of improving life in your town or village. (About 350 words)

2   Discuss the opinion that scientific experiments involving animals are never justified. (About 350 words)

3   You are to spend some time completely alone (on a desert island, in a space capsule etc.) and are allowed to take with you three things. What would you choose, and why? (About 350 words)

4   Using the information given in the following notes, write *two* contrasting statements of position, by (i) the chairman of the Paper Board and (ii) the trade union concerned. (About 150 words for each)

Major strike danger in nationalised paper industry.

12% increase in wages demanded in line with official arbitration.
9% recent compromise offer by Paper Board following original $6\frac{1}{2}$%.

Government subsidy not likely to be increased, and earmarked for essential machinery and modernisation.

---

5   Basing your answer on your reading of the prescribed text concerned, answer *one* of the following. (About 350 words)

SHAKESPEARE: *Macbeth*
Give some examples of the ways in which the special atmosphere of this play is created.

SCOTT FITZGERALD: *The Great Gatsby*
What does this novel tell us about American life in the 1920s?

ARNOLD WESKER: *Roots*

"Beatie: God in heaven, Ronnie. It does work, it's happening to me, I can feel it's happened ..."

What has happened to Beatie and how did it occur?

PAPER 3   USE OF ENGLISH   (2 hours)

SECTION A

1   *Fill each of the numbered blanks in the following passage with* **one** *suitable word.*

It is one of the oldest complaints that the young, at .... (1) the male young, are prone to crime, disorder and .... (2) kind of delinquency, and .... (3) some argue that this criminality is .... (4) to childish impulsiveness, others claim that it has come about .... (5) of the role .... (6) by the young in society. This role has changed from .... (7) it was in the past, since the young now tend to form a .... (8) apart from the .... (9) of society, with spending power far .... (10) what was available to earlier generations of youth. On the .... (11) hand, and this is particularly the .... (12) in the United States, their prospects .... (13) employment are much lower than .... (14) of adults. .... (15) numerous government training schemes, these prospects have been getting worse, and the trend is .... (16) greater youth unemployment. This, combined .... (17) the fact that parents are more uncertain and .... (18) prepared to exercise authority, has resulted .... (19) more crimes than ever .... (20) committed by young people.

2   *Finish each of the following sentences in such a way that it means exactly the same as the sentence printed before it.*

EXAMPLE: Immediately after his arrival, things went wrong.

ANSWER: No sooner *had he arrived than things went wrong.*

[34]

a) I applied for the job but was turned down.

   My ....

b) The Prime Minister was determined to remain in office.

   The Prime Minister had no ....

c) He said, "I wish I knew the answer."

   He said that ....

d) The refugees continued to feel unsafe until they had crossed the border.

   Not until ....

e) I don't know the first thing about aeronautics.

   I am ....

f) The students' riotous behaviour should have been severely punished.

   The students deserved ....

g) There are more people out of work in this country than ever before.

   Never ....

h) The chances are that the whole thing will have been forgotten by next term.

   In all ....

3   *Fill each of the blanks with a suitable word or phrase.*

   EXAMPLE: Even if I had stood on a chair, *I wouldn't have been able to reach the light bulb.*

a) You'd better be off .... my temper.

b) I know this restaurant is good but ....
   somewhere else?

c) I insisted .... even though she wanted to stay.

d) He makes a point .... all the doors before he goes out.

e) After many anxious hours .... upon the solution
   to the problem.

≫→

f)   If I .... the textbook from my friend, I would never have passed the test.

4   *For each of the sentences below, write a new sentence* **as similar as possible in meaning to the original sentence**, *but using the word given. This word must* **not be altered** *in any way.*

EXAMPLE: His arrival was completely unexpected.
          took

ANSWER: *His arrival took us completely by surprise.*

a)   He said he was anxious about the plight of the homeless.
     concern

     ....

b)   Their house has been broken into three times this year.
     had

     ....

c)   I would always do what you advised.
     advice

     ....

d)   He did the puzzle in two minutes.
     solution

     ....

e)   He owed his rescue to a passer-by.
     indebted

     ....

f)   There was not a single copy of the new book left in the shops.
     sell-out

     ....

g)   You must be on time for your interview.
     essential

     ....

h)   Only if you work hard now have you any chance of success.
     depends

     ....

[36]

SECTION B

5   *Read the following passage, then answer the questions which follow it.*

A newspaper can be said to have two chief functions: to disseminate information about current events at home and abroad, and to lead and shape public opinion. The principle was once expressed that "Comment is free but facts are sacred". This enshrines the assumption that "facts" can be reported with complete objectivity. That this is not so is widely recognised in practice.   5
The very process of selecting which items to include and determining the prominence to be given to those items, in terms of their position in the paper as a whole and on the individual pages, decisions about typography and illustration, all reflect conscious or unconscious editorial choice. The editor has, however, to satisfy his readers, at least to the extent that they continue   10
to buy the paper; he is answerable also to the proprietors and subject to the informed criticism of commentators in the weekly reviews presented in other publications, on the radio or on television. He must, therefore, be able to justify the choices he makes and this obviously limits his subjectivity. There is never complete objectivity and impersonality in any written record, but   15
merely differing degrees of objectivity and impersonality. The two extremes may be illustrated by the short news item, reported straight, and the assertion of opinion in the leader, which explicitly seeks to influence and even shape public opinion.

Editorial choice and assessment, exercised through selection and com-   20
mentary, can help the reader to assess and evaluate the information made available to him. Nevertheless, the brevity of many articles, and the sensationalisation and personalisation of news so characteristic of the "popular dailies" (e.g. *The Daily Express, Daily Mail, Daily Mirror* and *The Sun*) often leave the reader confused and incapable of distinguishing between   25
the trivial and the important. He is thus less able to appreciate the real significance of what is reported. In these publications flare-ups of violence are frequently described in a highly dramatic fashion, whereas ongoing situations, precisely because they are not dramatic or sensational, are not considered to be "newsworthy" and hence go unreported. By contrast, the   30
vast coverage and all-inclusive accounts of events provided by the so-called "quality" newspapers such as *The Daily Telegraph, The Guardian* and *The Times* make them virtually unreadable in the course of a normal working day.

Nearly all newspaper copy has to be written at great speed. There is no time for prolonged drafting, revision and polishing. Consequently, the   35
language of journalism tends to be looser, less accurate and more frequently incorrect than that used in other forms of printed prose. This sometimes also leads to weaknesses in the organisation of the material. The speed of writing, and the journalistic practice of presenting pieces of information in order of importance so that the editor can reduce the length of a story by cutting it   40
from the end backwards in accordance with the amount of space he has available, determine together the peculiar organisational structure of news

items. On the other hand, this speed means that journalism is the written style closest to the spoken form of the language.

a) Explain in your own words what the passage says are the main functions of a newspaper.

   ....

   ....

b) What is meant by the phrase "Comment is free but facts are sacred" (lines 3 and 4)?

   ....

   ....

c) What, according to the author, is "widely recognised in practice" (line 5)?

   ....

d) In what ways can newspaper editors influence the coverage and presentation of news?

   ....

   ....

   ....

e) In what way is a newspaper editor said to be dependent on his readers?

   ....

f) What are the "two extremes" referred to in line 16?

   ....

   ....

g) Explain the meaning of the phrase "reported straight" in line 17.

   ....

h) Which features of popular newspapers often make it difficult for the reader to understand the importance of the events they report?

....

....

....

i) Give an alternative expression for the phrase "flare-ups of violence" in line 27.

....

j) Why are newspapers like *The Daily Telegraph*, *The Guardian* and *The Times* said to be "virtually unreadable in the course of a normal working day"?

....

k) Why is journalistic language likely to be less correct than other forms of printed prose?

....

l) What is "peculiar" (line 42) about the way news reports are compiled?

....

....

m) In a paragraph of 70–100 words, summarise the factors which, according to the author of the passage, determine the style and content of newspaper articles.

....

....

....

....

....

....

PAPER 4 LISTENING COMPREHENSION
(about 30 minutes)

FIRST PART

1 The speaker mentions **three** disadvantages of using bark and sisal ropes to join timber. What are they? Write your answers in the boxes.

(i)

(ii)

(iii)

2 The first method of joint-making that the speaker recommends involves cutting a pole. Which of these four drawings shows what the end of the pole would look like **after** it has been cut? Put a tick in one of the boxes A, B, C or D.

A   B   C   D

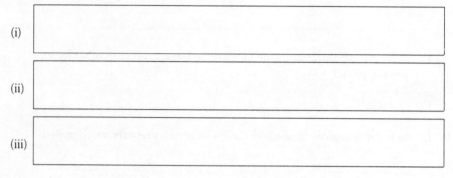

3 Which of these joints does the speaker describe as strong and cheap? Put a tick in one of the boxes A, B, C or D.

A   B   C   D

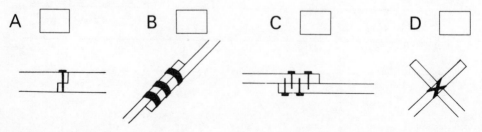

[40]

4 *This drawing represents the second type of joint that the speaker recommends. Write the names of the different parts in the boxes beside each one. One has been done for you.*

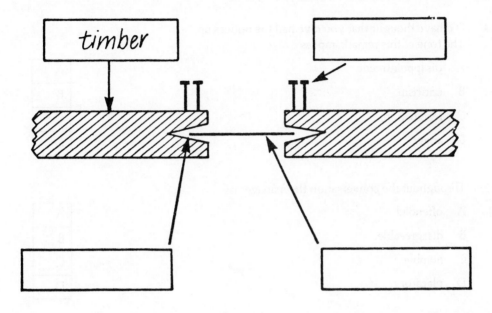

SECOND PART

For questions 5–10 fill in the missing information in the spaces provided.

AIRLINE	DESTINATION	FLIGHT NO	GATE NO
British Caledonian	(5)	BR 907	(6) ....
Dan-Air	TEL-AVIV	384044	(7) ....
British Caledonian	LAGOS	(8)	19
British Caledonian	(9)	BR 886	(10) ....

THIRD PART

For questions 11–13 tick one of the boxes A, B, C or D.

11   "I'd have thought that you'd've had the notices up."
      The tone of this remark implies

      A   disappointment.

      B   criticism.

      C   resignation.

      D   anger.

| A |
| B |
| C |
| D |

12   Throughout the conversation the manager is

      A   offended.

      B   disagreeable.

      C   humble.

      D   placatory.

| A |
| B |
| C |
| D |

13   "Is there no self-determination these days?" The woman expects

      A   the answer yes.

      B   the answer no.

      C   no answer at all.

      D   an explanation.

| A |
| B |
| C |
| D |

FOURTH PART

For questions 14–19 tick whether you think the statements about Attlee are true.

	Yes	No
14 He had great political ambitions as a young man.		
15 He had an ordinary education.		
16 Politics was the only profession he ever had.		
17 He became a Socialist before World War One.		
18 He was more capable than other politicians.		
19 He is a very well-known person in British History.		

PAPER 5   INTERVIEW   (15–20 minutes)

You will be asked to take part in a conversation with a group of other students or with your teacher. The conversation will be based on one particular topic area or theme, for example holidays, work, food.

Of course each interview will be different for each student or group of students, but a *typical* interview is described below.

★ At the start of the interview you will be asked to talk about one of the photographs among the Interview Exercises at the back of the book.

★ You will then be asked to discuss one of the passages at the back of the book. Your teacher may ask you to talk about its content, where you think it comes from, who the author or speaker is, whether you agree or disagree with it, and so on. You will *not* be asked to read the passage aloud, but you may quote parts of it to make your point.

★ You may then be asked to discuss for example an advertisement, a leaflet, extract from a newspaper etc. Your teacher will tell you which of the Interview Exercises to look at.

★ You may also be asked to take part in an activity with a group of other students or your teacher. Your teacher will tell you which section among the Interview Exercises you should look at.

Practice Test 3

PAPER 1   READING COMPREHENSION   (1 hour)

Answer all questions. Indicate your choice of answer in every case **on the separate answer sheet** *already given out, which should show your name and examination index number. Follow carefully the instructions about how to record your answers. Give* **one answer only** *to each question. Marks will not be deducted for wrong answers: your total score on this test will be the number of correct answers you give.*

SECTION A

In this section you must choose the word or phrase which best completes each sentence. **On your answer sheet** *indicate the letter A, B, C or D against the number of each item 1 to 25 for the word or phrase you choose.*

1   The Government's present policy is seen as a .... to local democracy.
    A threat   B harm   C suppression   D sneer

2   Sport provides an .... for a teenager's feelings of aggression or frustration.
    A overflow   B exit   C outlet   D exhaust

3   Under the circumstances it .... be best to wait for a few weeks.
    A seemed   B ought   C might   D should

4   My throat infection left me very .... and made talking difficult.
    A hoarse   B dumb   C inarticulate   D speechless

5   .... all my efforts, I will not have the report ready by Friday.
    A Making   B No matter   C Considering   D Despite

6   The fumes were so thick that she was .... for breath.
    A suffocating   B gasping   C inhaling   D wheezing

7   Before the group of doctors would give their opinion they wanted to ....
    with each other.
    A confess   B confirm   C confer   D confide

8   He clearly had no .... of doing any work, although it was only a week till the
    exam.
    A desire   B ambition   C willingness   D intention

9   The staff at the hospital were well .... to deal with the epidemic.
    A capable   B equal   C ready   D equipped

10 An application to join this scheme places you under no obligation ....
    A indeed   B eventually   C apart   D whatsoever

11 Enough money has been raised to .... the hospital's survival.
    A ensure   B endow   C enable   D empower

12 An architect planning a new house should always .... in mind his client's
    needs.
    A carry   B take   C train   D bear

13 The two men looked so alike that it was impossible to .... between them.
    A distinguish   B differ   C discern   D discriminate

14 Whenever she catches a cold, she gets a .... all over her face.
    A lump   B rash   C blemish   D sore

15 At that time our only hope of success .... in recruiting extra help.
    A lay   B arose   C resided   D stood

16 As he made no .... to our quarrel, I assumed he had forgiven me.
    A statement   B mention   C reference   D comment

17 I'm not sure why he didn't go into the higher class, but I .... he failed the
    entrance test.
    A estimate   B suspect   C predict   D deduce

18 He pretended to be an Englishman, but his foreign accent gave him ....
    A away   B off   C out   D up

19 I recognise his face, but his name .... me.
    A escapes   B deludes   C fails   D misses

20 The new sports centre .... for all kinds of leisure activities.
    A deals   B supplies   C furnishes   D caters

21 They threw petrol on to the bonfire and the sudden .... lit up the whole
    garden.
    A glow   B twinkle   C spark   D flare

22 Nobody .... out much hope of finding the missing climbers alive.
    A holds   B keeps   C puts   D finds

23 The Government has decided to spend billions of dollars on yet ....
    agricultural subsidies.
    A extra   B other   C more   D additional

24 I know William has been disobedient, but don't be too .... on him.
    A heavy   B strong   C hard   D strict

25 Computer technology will bring .... a revolution in business administration.
    A over   B across   C up   D about

SECTION B

In this section you will find after each of the passages a number of questions or unfinished statements about the passage, each with four suggested answers or ways of finishing. You must choose the one which you think fits best according to the passage. **On your answer sheet,** *indicate the letter A, B, C or D against the number of each item 26 to 40 for the answer you choose. Give* **one answer only** *to each question. Read each passage right through before choosing your answers.*

FIRST PASSAGE

My mother used to go to the South of France in order to paint. Her style had deepened into something altogether richer than before, a sternly unaffected impressionism. The strength of her pictures was also, to my mind, their limitation, which is another way of saying she had personality. Everything she painted had behind it a very acute temperament, both serene and warm. More heart and instinct than thought had gone into her work. To paint what she saw was enough for her. What she felt would inevitably follow.

She strode across the paintable landscape, an old straw hat on her head, sniffing out the best angles and compositions, while Frieda and I followed like native porters in a movie, carrying canvases and easels and boxes of paints. It was a curious way of spending vacations, since there was nothing I could do but paint as well, although for me to paint what I saw was never satisfying. I could not bring myself to aim for a mere faithful reproduction, nor did any work without comment, without an edge, interest me for long. Once I remember the astonishment of both my mother and Frieda when, at the end of a smouldering day in the hills behind the village, I showed them my painting, the subject of which was a post-Christmas sale at a large department store in London.

This event became the pretext for a family joke, which was brought out on every and any occasion, and I hope I laughed with as good a grace every time I heard it. The fact was that I did not consider it much of a pastime for a boy away from school to be sitting before a landscape nature had put together with great competence, and to seek to reproduce it on a small piece of paper. In case it be thought that a note of self-pity has crept into this account of my apparent boredom, I must say that the intention was never to complain about my fate, but merely to explain the form of my protest. A Christmas sale in a department store should have been enough to convince anybody that I had no ambitions to be a landscape painter, but, no, it was taken, told and retold as evidence of youthful spirits in someone who would no doubt settle later on, and I, social animal that I was, laughed with the others and gave credence to the myth.

26　Why did the author like his mother's painting?
    A　He thought it showed her strength of character.
    B　He realised she took painting seriously.
    C　She did not think about what she was painting.
    D　She had a stronger personality than he had.

27　When she was choosing a place to paint, the author's mother
    A　tried to find a shady spot.
    B　considered the possibilities carefully.
    C　found it difficult to make up her mind.
    D　had to consider all her equipment.

28　Why did the author's painting surprise his mother and Frieda?
    A　It seemed out of keeping with the environment.
    B　They didn't know he'd been to a Christmas sale.
    C　It was a strange subject for a boy.
    D　He didn't usually paint in that style.

29　Why did the author paint a picture of a post-Christmas sale?
    A　He only had a small sheet of paper.
    B　He was too young for landscape painting.
    C　He was determined to show off his skill.
    D　He wanted to make his opinion clear.

30　When his parents told the story of the strange painting, the author laughed because
    A　he wanted to join in with everyone else.
    B　he thought it was a funny story.
    C　he alone knew the truth.
    D　the story improved with retelling.

SECOND PASSAGE

The diseases afflicting Western societies have undergone dramatic changes. In the course of a century, so many mass killers have vanished that two-thirds of all deaths are now associated with the diseases of old age. Those who die young are more often than not the victims of accidents, violence and suicide.

    These changes in public health are generally equated with progress and are attributed to more or better medical care. In fact, there is no evidence of any direct relation between changing disease patterns and the so-called progress of medicine.

The impotence of medical services to change life expectancy and the insignificance of much contemporary clinical care in the curing of disease are all obvious, well-documented – and well-repressed.

Neither the proportion of doctors in a population, nor the clinical tools at their disposal, nor the number of hospital beds, are causal factors in the striking changes in overall patterns of disease. The new techniques available to recognise and treat such conditions as pernicious anaemia and hypertension, or to correct congenital malformations by surgical interventions, increase our understanding of disease but do not reduce its incidence. The fact that there are more doctors where certain diseases have become rare has little to do with their ability to control or eliminate them. It simply means that doctors deploy themselves as they like, more so than other professionals, and that they tend to gather where the climate is healthy, where the water is clean, and where people work and can pay for their services.

31 The diseases that prevail in contemporary Western societies
    A result from modern life styles.
    B kill many people at once.
    C are concentrated among the elderly.
    D resist the latest drugs.

32 The writer claims that evidence of medicine's inadequacies
    A has been kept quiet.
    B is widely accepted.
    C has been destroyed.
    D should not be publicised.

33 The author thinks that the presence of large numbers of doctors in a community
    A does not have much effect on disease.
    B disguises the true facts about disease.
    C controls the spread of disease.
    D improves the overall quality of life.

34 Many doctors choose to live where
    A research facilities are available.
    B they are most needed.
    C they can be near colleagues.
    D conditions discourage disease.

35 What is the author's attitude to developments in medicine?
    A matter-of-fact
    B cautious
    C indifferent
    D cynical

THIRD PASSAGE

A
Twenty-five years ago this month the Soviet Union put the first Sputnik into orbit. The Space Age began. What now is the legacy of the quarter century? If I can put it in one word, it is globalism. Forced into our unwilling minds has been a view that presents humanity as a single entity. This has been done in several ways.

B
Material: as a result of the satellites that have been put into orbit, Earth has become a unit. Communication satellites have put every portion of the world into direct and virtually instantaneous touch with every other. This has developed worldwide business and diplomacy to the point where returning to the way things were before 1957 is unthinkable.

C
Psychological: the sight of the Earth as a whole, a planetary sphere, seen small and skyborne from the Moon, forces us to think of it as small and fragile. It makes less sensible the arbitrary division of its surface into portions that we must think of as sacred. The probes that have gone well beyond the Moon have revealed planetary dots in the sky to be worlds. We have stared at the craters of Mercury, the highlands of Venus, the dead volcanoes of Mars and the living ones of Io, the swirling storms of Jupiter and the intricate rings of Saturn. We cannot see all of this without feeling that Earth is part of an enormously greater whole, and that parcelling out the dust-speck we live on into mutually hostile sub-dust-specks is worse than mad. It is ridiculous.

D
Potential: the first quarter century of the Space Age has brought us to the brink of being able to turn exploration into settlement. The United States has the space shuttle, a vehicle that can be re-used repeatedly to bring material into orbit. The Soviet Union has kept its cosmonauts in space for six months at a time and shown that they can live and work without ill effects. It is now planning a space station that can be put into orbit to make use of the unusual properties of space.

36 Which paragraph states that the advances of the last 25 years cannot be reversed?
     A   B   C   D

37 Which paragraph attempts to make the Space Age sound romantic?
     A   B   C   D

38 Which paragraph mentions the future possibilities of space research?
     A   B   C   D

39 Which paragraph mocks outdated attitudes?
     A   B   C   D

40 Which paragraph summarises the writer's opinion?
     A   B   C   D

[50]

PAPER 2   COMPOSITION   (2 hours)

*Write **two only** of the following composition exercises. Your answers must follow exactly the instructions given. Write in pen, not pencil. You are allowed to make alterations, but see that your work is clear and easy to read.*

1   Describe the perfect secretary, parent, politician or teacher. (About 350 words)

2   "Computers threaten the privacy of the individual." Discuss. (About 350 words)

3   Write a story entitled "The Coincidence". (About 350 words)

4   You want to establish *one* of the following. Write a letter to an estate agent giving a detailed description of the kind of premises you would find most suitable. (About 300 words)

> a travel agency
> a health studio
> a riding school

5   Basing your answer on your reading of the prescribed text concerned, answer *one* of the following. (About 350 words)

GEORGE ELIOT: *Silas Marner*
What effect did the arrival of Eppie have on Silas Marner's life?

ROBERT GRAVES: *Goodbye To All That*
What were the advantages and disadvantages of belonging to Graves's particular regiment?

MARGARET DRABBLE: *The Millstone*
Why is the book called "The Millstone"?

PAPER 3 USE OF ENGLISH (2 hours)

SECTION A

1 *Fill each of the numbered blanks in the following passage with* **one** *suitable word.*

A child beginning to play for the first time with children who speak a different language begins to make the sounds which they make without waiting to learn why, ... (1) as he learns to hide himself or run .... (2) chased. In a very .... (3) time he .... (4) learnt the meanings of the words .... (5) using them in the right place at the right .... (6). Yet many teachers .... (7) to think that a child can use .... (8) sentence in a foreign language .... (9) has not .... (10) carefully explained and accounted .... (11). If we learn a language .... (12) part of behaviour, as inconceivable .... (13) its own as the flower is inconceivable .... (14) the plant, we can learn words .... (15) expressions, and work them .... (16) our knowledge of .... (17) language, without necessarily understanding .... (18) what they mean. Our suddenly realising, ... (19) day, that we know what they mean .... (20) a sign that we know them.

2 *Finish each of the following sentences in such a way that it means exactly the same as the sentence printed before it.*

    EXAMPLE: I expect that he will get there by lunchtime.

    ANSWER: I expect him *to get there by lunchtime.*

a) "Please don't drive so fast!" Ann begged her boyfriend.

    Ann pleaded ....

b) Despite his ungainly air he is remarkably agile.

    Although ....

c) She is proud of being such a good cook.

    She prides ....

d) My protests were ignored.

    Nobody ....

e) I'm sure he took your briefcase by mistake.

    I'm sure he didn't ....

f) We only despatch goods after receiving the money.

    Only after the money ....

g) You pay £20 a month for a period of one year.

    You pay in twelve successive ....

h) He'll settle down. Then his performance will improve.

    Once ....

3 *Fill each of the blanks with a suitable word or phrase.*

    EXAMPLE: Even if I had stood on a chair, *I wouldn't have been able to* reach the light bulb.

a) You only started this job an hour ago: surely you .... already?

b) There is a fair .... work left to do.

»»→

c) Their wedding was in June 1961. By this time next year .... twenty-five years.

d) Move your car, please. Parking .... here.

e) Mrs Jones is .... you could ever wish to meet.

f) If I had known you weren't coming I .... to such trouble.

g) He would sooner .... than by boat.

h) Stop teasing that dog. If you get bitten it .... right.

4   *For each of the sentences below, write a new sentence* **as similar as possible in meaning to the original sentence,** *but using the word given. This word must* **not be altered** *in any way.*

     EXAMPLE: John inflated the tyres of his bicycle.
        blew

     ANSWER: *John blew up the tyres of his bicycle.*

a) He will not be put off by their comments.
deter

....

b) She complains far too often for my liking.
frequent

....

c) Some people accept that nuclear war is inevitable.
resigned

....

d) I find his handwriting very hard to read.
difficulty

....

e) The fridge is completely empty.
left

....

f) Money is of little value on a desert island.
   counts

   ....

g) Can you tell me where the Midland Hotel is?
   direct

   ....

h) The Prime Minister felt it appropriate to make a statement.
   fit

   ....

SECTION B

5 *Read the following passage, then answer the questions which follow it.*

"Let me," cried Shakespeare's Julius Caesar, "have men about me that are fat, sleek-headed men, and such as sleep o' nights." One can see his point. There is something infinitely reassuring about a rounded, even cherubic, countenance; something sound and trustworthy about a man of bulk.

Now this may, of course, be merely an optical illusion. But the lean and hungry look does not, in general, inspire confidence. Perhaps that's why, when a fat man is proved to be a villain, he's very villainous indeed. We feel sadly let down. 5

Ramblings such as this occurred to me in considering the case of the television presenter. In recent weeks the nature of my work has brought me face to face with many forms of the genus interlocutor. As you know, they come in many shapes and sizes. Any consideration of their merits must begin with the visual impression that they make. Let us disregard the disembodied ones, the out-of-vision narrators, those known in the trade as "voice-overs". Our business is with the front men and women in corporeal view, upon whom the producer pins all his hopes of an audience joining and staying with his product. And, while it's a television truism that the strength of a chat-show or a magazine is often the strength of its weakest link, it's equally true that a presenter can make or mar the best-intentioned programme. 10 15

It is no easy task. Far too often presenters and producers forget that the Box is essentially an intimate medium. It is not a market place, nor a Speaker's Corner. And, as in those two public arenas, the louder the voice, the more strident the appeal, the more dubious appear the goods for sale. No, your good presenter must get on intimate terms with his viewer – singular, not plural. He may in numerical terms be talking to millions, but it is still a one-to-one business. 20 25

So, the essence of the craft is the quiet, conversational button-holing of the viewer. This is precisely the point at which good T.V. presentation parts company with show business. Introducing the next item or personality in a steady crescendo of spurious excitement is no more than rabble-rousing, to 30 elicit audience applause. Often what follows falls flat on its face, despite the bolstering of audience reaction, for the viewer at home, solitary before his set.

The ground rules of presentation are pretty obvious – a friendly face and manner, a persona one can like on first impression or warm to as the one-way 35 conversation continues. It was no accident that the archetypal presenter, Richard Dimbleby, was so good at his job. He was a large man, voice and personality projected effortlessly into the home. Always the key-note was a quiet sincerity. In a lighter fashion, the ever-green Cliff Michelmore continues the tradition. He's another rounded person, in several senses, with whom 40 the viewer finds instant rapport. Of course, there are dangers in the large personality. It can be allowed to grow so that it fills the screen, allowing only a peep over the shoulder of the famous front-man at what the programme's really about.

a) In your own words explain the meaning of the sentence "One can see his point" (line 2).

....

....

b) What is the "optical illusion" referred to in line 5?

....

....

c) Why should a fat, villainous man be "very villainous indeed" (line 7)?

....

....

d) What does "ramblings" (line 9) mean, and why is it appropriate here?

....

....

....

e) How can an interlocutor be "disembodied" (line 14)?

....

....

f) What trade is referred to by the phrase "in the trade" (line 14)?

....

g) What does the phrase "his product" (line 17) refer to?

....

h) What are the two public arenas referred to by the writer (line 22)?

....

i) What effect does a loud voice often have on an audience, according to the writer?

....

....

j) Explain in your own words the phrase "a crescendo of spurious excitement" (line 30).

....

....

k) What is the effect on the viewer of the "rabble-rousing" mentioned in line 30?

....

l) What is the "one-way conversation" referred to in lines 35–6?

....

m) What do you gather from the passage there is in common between Richard Dimbleby and Cliff Michelmore?

....

....

n) In 50–60 words summarise the writer's views on how a television presenter should approach his job, and the ways in which he could go wrong.

....

....

....

....

....

....

....

....

....

....

PAPER 4   LISTENING COMPREHENSION
(about 30 minutes)

FIRST PART

1   *Tick whether you think the statements are true or false.*

	True	False

Football
a)   Tonight's football match was dull.

b)   Leeds beat Liverpool.

Sailing
c)   Tracy Burton is 14.

d)   Tracy Burton started her voyage today.

Athletics
e)   Finland won the men's events.

f)   Finland won the women's events.

Cycling
g)   The result was a surprise.

h)   There was a close finish.

SECOND PART

For questions 2–4 put a tick in one of the boxes A, B, C or D.

2   Why does the occupant of the house keep saying sorry?

   A   She is apologising.

   B   She is being defensive.

   C   She is expressing anger.

   D   She is attempting to refuse.

A
B
C
D ✗

3   How does the occupant view the offer of free samples?

   A   with enthusiasm

   B   with disappointment

   C   with reluctance

   D   with surprise

A
B
C ✗
D

4   Elizabeth Brown, the interviewer, is

   A   persistent.

   B   bullying.

   C   reserved.

   D   angry.

A ✗
B
C
D

THIRD PART

For questions 5–7 put a tick in **one** *of the boxes A, B, C or D next to the correct picture.*

5   Which of the maps shows the exact location of the accident?

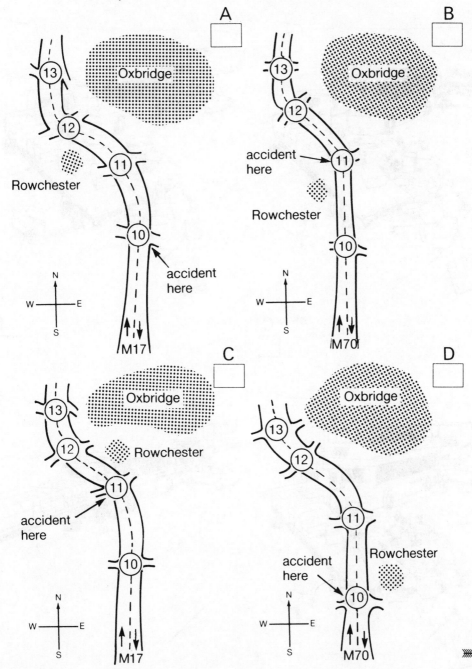

6   Which picture correctly illustrates the accident?

A

B

C

D

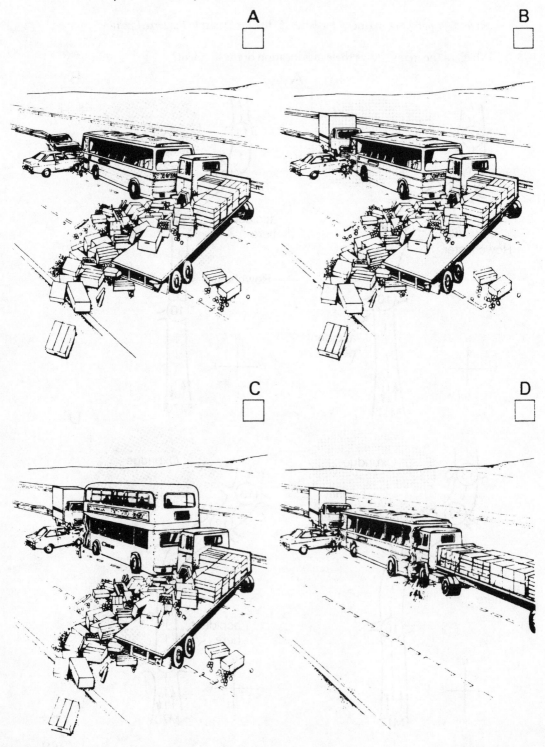

7   Which of the maps shows the diversion suggested in the announcement?

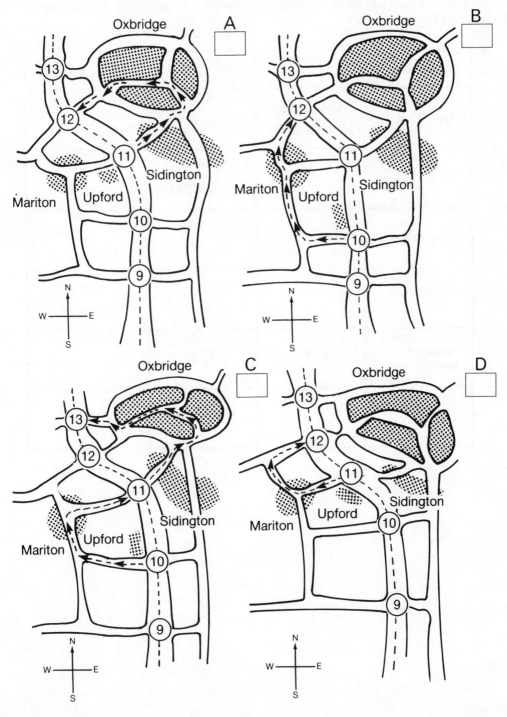

FOURTH PART

For question 8 you must complete the missing information on the table below. Some of it has been filled in for you.

8

Job Number	1	2	3
Type of Job	Heavy goods Vehicle fitter		
Pay		to be arranged	
Hours of Work			
Qualifications			none necessary
Reference Number	1419	1435	
Telephone Number		the same	the same

PAPER 5   INTERVIEW   (15–20 minutes)

You will be asked to take part in a conversation with a group of other students
or with your teacher. The conversation will be based on one particular topic
area or theme, for example holidays, work, food.

Of course each interview will be different for each student or group of students,
but a *typical* interview is described below.

★ At the start of the interview you will be asked to talk about one of the
   photographs among the Interview Exercises at the back of the book.

★ You will then be asked to discuss one of the passages at the back of the book.
   Your teacher may ask you to talk about its content, where you think it comes
   from, who the author or speaker is, whether you agree or disagree with it,
   and so on. You will *not* be asked to read the passage aloud, but you may
   quote parts of it to make your point.

★ You may then be asked to discuss for example an advertisement, a leaflet,
   extract from a newspaper etc. Your teacher will tell you which of the
   Interview Exercises to look at.

★ You may also be asked to take part in an activity with a group of other
   students or your teacher. Your teacher will tell you which section among the
   Interview Exercises you should look at.

Practice Test 4

PAPER 1   READING COMPREHENSION   (1 hour)

Answer all questions. Indicate your choice of answer in every case **on the separate answer
sheet** *already given out, which should show your name and examination index number.
Follow carefully the instructions about how to record your answers. Give* **one answer only** *to
each question. Marks will not be deducted for wrong answers: your total score on this test will
be the number of correct answers you give.*

SECTION A

In this section you must choose the word or phrase which best completes each sentence. **On
your answer sheet** *indicate the letter A, B, C or D against the number of each item 1 to 25
for the word or phrase you choose.*

1   It was not easy to understand her .... to the situation.
    A feelings   B conduct   C outlook   D reaction

2   Do very young children really .... foreign travel?
    A appreciate   B benefit   C delight   D evaluate

3   Students sometimes support themselves by .... of evening jobs.
    A ways   B means   C efforts   D methods

4   One way of cutting down waste is to .... such things as glass and paper.
    A repeat   B renew   C recycle   D redirect

5   A glass of wine now and then won't .... you any harm.
    A make   B do   C take   D give

6   Automation in factories has made many .... workers redundant.
    A fabrication   B hand   C manual   D manufacturing

7   When he heard how well the new company was doing, he took a calculated
    .... and invested all his money in it.
    A venture   B opportunity   C chance   D risk

8   A strike in the mining industry is .... to bring about a shortage of coal in the
    near future.
    A causing   B resulting   C threatening   D proposing

9   I'd prefer to postpone that decision .... I hear from my uncle.
    A before   B except   C in case   D in spite

10 Frank would be more popular in the office if he didn't try so hard to ....
    himself with the boss.
    A ingratiate   B sympathise   C congratulate   D regard

11 The local wine is rather rough, but you'll soon .... a taste for it!
    A receive   B acquire   C accept   D adopt

12 He was too busy to give the document more .... attention.
    A exact   B careful   C precise   D accurate

13 The burglar's presence was betrayed by a .... floorboard.
    A cracking   B crunching   C groaning   D creaking

14 A few jokes always .... up a lecture.
    A raise   B inspire   C liven   D loosen

15 It was felt that he lacked the .... to pursue a difficult task to the very end.
    A persuasion   B commitment   C engagement   D obligation

16 It was found that the diet of older people is often .... in vitamins.
    A short   B inadequate   C deficient   D failing

17 The chairman asked members to .... their votes for or against the proposal.
    A bid   B offer   C cast   D throw

18 The case for an increase in spending on education has been proved beyond the
    .... of a doubt.
    A shadow   B hesitation   C suspicion   D shade

19 This museum has more visitors than .... any other in the world.
    A really   B practically   C actually   D utterly

20 All the information was .... alphabetically in large cabinets.
    A filed   B gathered   C composed   D crammed

21 This course .... no previous knowledge of the subject.
    A assumes   B assigns   C assures   D assembles

22 Although they had only been invited for lunch they .... until suppertime.
    A stayed on   B stayed out   C stayed up   D stayed in

23 It should be .... that students are expected to attend classes regularly.
    A marked   B reminded   C noted   D perceived

>>>→

[67]

24 He was barred from the club for refusing to .... with the rules.
   A conform   B abide   C adhere   D comply

25 That ancient car of his is a .... joke among his friends.
   A steady   B standing   C settled   D stable

SECTION B

In this section you will find after each of the passages a number of questions or unfinished statements about the passage, each with four suggested answers or ways of finishing. You must choose the one which you think fits best according to the passage. **On your answer sheet** *indicate the letter A, B, C or D against the number of each item 26 to 40 for the answer you choose. Give* **one answer only** *to each question. Read each passage right through before choosing your answers.*

FIRST PASSAGE

Drunken driving – sometimes called America's socially accepted form of murder – has become a national epidemic. Every hour of every day about three Americans on average are killed by drunken drivers, adding up to an incredible 250,000 over the past decade.

A drunken driver is usually defined as one with a 0.10 blood alcohol content or roughly three beers, glasses of wine or shots of whisky drunk within two hours. Heavy drinking used to be an acceptable part of the American macho image and judges were lenient in most courts, but the drunken slaughter has recently caused so many well-publicised tragedies, especially involving young children, that public opinion is no longer so tolerant.

Twenty states have raised the legal drinking age to 21, reversing a trend in the 1960s to reduce it to 18. After New Jersey lowered it to 18, the number of people killed by 18–20-year-old drivers more than doubled, so the state recently upped it back to 21.

Reformers, however, fear raising the drinking age will have little effect unless accompanied by educational programmes to help young people to develop "responsible attitudes" about drinking and teach them to resist peer pressure to drink.

Tough new laws have led to increased arrests and tests and, in many areas already, to a marked decline in fatalities. Some states are also penalising bars for serving customers too many drinks. A tavern in Massachusetts was fined for serving six or more double brandies to a customer who was "obviously intoxicated" and later drove off the road, killing a nine-year-old boy.

As the fatalities continue to occur daily in every state, some Americans are even beginning to speak well of the 13 years of national prohibition of alcohol that began in 1919, what President Hoover called the "noble experiment". They forget that legal prohibition didn't stop drinking, but encouraged political corruption and organised crime. As with the booming drug trade generally, there is no easy solution.

26 Drunken driving has become a major problem in America because
    A   most Americans are heavy drinkers.
    B   Americans are now less shocked by road accidents.
    C   accidents attract so much publicity.
    D   drinking is a socially accepted habit in America.

27 Why has public opinion regarding drunken driving changed?
    A   Detailed statistics are now available.
    B   The news media have highlighted the problem.
    C   Judges are giving more severe sentences.
    D   Drivers are more conscious of their image.

28 Statistics issued in New Jersey suggested that
    A   many drivers were not of legal age.
    B   young drivers were often bad drivers.
    C   the level of drinking increased in the 1960s.
    D   the legal drinking age should be raised.

29 Laws recently introduced in some states have
    A   reduced the number of convictions.
    B   resulted in fewer serious accidents.
    C   prevented bars from serving drunken customers.
    D   specified the amount drivers can drink.

30 Why is the problem of drinking and driving difficult to solve?
    A   Alcohol is easily obtained.
    B   Drinking is linked to organised crime.
    C   Legal prohibition has already failed.
    D   Legislation alone is not sufficient.

SECOND PASSAGE

Reading to oneself is a modern activity which was almost unknown to the scholars of the classical and medieval worlds, while during the fifteenth century the term "reading" undoubtedly meant reading aloud. Only during the nineteenth century did silent reading become commonplace.

One should be wary, however, of assuming that silent reading came about simply because reading aloud is a distraction to others. Examination of factors related to the historical development of silent reading reveals that it became the usual mode of reading for most adult reading tasks mainly because the tasks themselves changed in character.

The last century saw a steady gradual increase in literacy, and thus in the number of readers. As readers increased, so the number of potential listeners declined, and thus there was some reduction in the need to read aloud. As reading for the benefit of listeners grew less common, so came the flourishing of reading as a private activity in such public places as libraries, railway carriages and offices, where reading aloud would cause distraction to other readers.

Towards the end of the century there was still considerable argument over whether books should be used for information or treated respectfully, and over whether the reading of material such as newspapers was in some way mentally weakening. Indeed this argument remains with us still in education. However, whatever its virtues, the old shared literacy culture had gone and was replaced by the printed mass media on the one hand and by books and periodicals for a specialised readership on the other.

By the end of the century students were being recommended to adopt attitudes to books and to use skills in reading them which were inappropriate, if not impossible, for the oral reader. The social, cultural, and technological changes in the century had greatly altered what the term "reading" implied.

31 Why was reading aloud common before the nineteenth century?
    A   Silent reading had not been discovered.
    B   There were few places available for private reading.
    C   Few people could read for themselves.
    D   People relied on reading for entertainment.

32 The development of silent reading during the nineteenth century indicated
    A   a change in the status of literate people.
    B   a change in the nature of reading.
    C   an increase in the number of books.
    D   an increase in the average age of readers.

33 Educationalists are still arguing about
    A   the importance of silent reading.
    B   the amount of information yielded by books and newspapers.
    C   the effects of reading on health.
    D   the value of different types of reading material.

34 The emergence of the mass media and of specialised periodicals showed that
    A   standards of literacy had declined.
    B   readers' interests had diversified.
    C   printing techniques had improved.
    D   educationalists' attitudes had changed.

35 What is the writer of this passage attempting to do?
    A   explain how present-day reading habits developed
    B   change people's attitudes to reading
    C   show how reading methods have improved
    D   encourage the growth of reading

THIRD PASSAGE

Extract 1

The 20th century is the age of mechanisation, mass production, electrification and automation. More women go out to work and less baking is done at home. For many, the factory loaf provides a convenient answer to today's needs as it is wrapped and sliced ready to use. However, although one would not really wish to bring back the so-called "good old days", it would be satisfying to bring back the good things associated with times gone by, such as the slower pace of life, fresh flavoursome food and home baking. Breadmaking is one of the basics and also one of the most rewarding aspects of home baking. Do not be inhibited by the aura surrounding it: once mastered, breadmaking is simple.

Extract 2

Today, over 80% of the bread sold in Britain is produced in factories. It's soft and white and handily wrapped. All but about 5% of the rest is made with the same characterless flour, supplied by the milling monopolies which control our bread industry. So wherever it comes from, it all tastes much the same. A revolt against this dismal standardisation is now gathering momentum. All over the country people are again making their own bread. Indeed, the author has been doing so for about fifteen years.

Extract 3

EAT MORE BREAD
It's cheap. It's nourishing!

Nowhere in the great wheat-producing countries of the world can you buy good, fresh, wholesome bread as cheaply as you can in Britain. It is baked in spotlessly clean bakeries by skilled bakers who know how to make bread light, delicious and nourishing. Eat more white or brown bread; it is all highly nutritious and recommended by the best medical authorities.

Extract 4

I determined to have a try at baking. My cookery book was discouraging, making it seem that to cook a loaf of bread was like carrying out some chemical experiment. With beginner's luck, I produced some lovely rolls. These were placed on the table within reach of Arthur at dinner.

"Good roll, this," he said, trying one. "Where did you get them? A new baker?"

"Yes," I said, as casually as my bursting pride would allow me, "I made them myself." "Do you mean to tell me," he exclaimed, "that this thing is only flour and water?" Holding it up in amazement, he added, "Then what on earth do they do to the bread in the shops?"

36   Extracts 1 and 2 differ on the subject of
    A   the convenience of commercial bread.
    B   the quality of home-baked bread.
    C   the present trend in home baking.
    D   the origins of most modern bread.

37   Extract 3 contradicts the first two extracts by stating that commercial bread is
    A   cheap.
    B   light.
    C   delicious.
    D   nutritious.

≫→

38 The first three extracts all agree that bread should be
    A   convenient.
    B   nourishing.
    C   fresh.
    D   tasty.

39 The writer of extract 4
    A   agrees with extract 3.
    B   supports the criticism of commercial bread.
    C   emphasises the health value of home-baked bread.
    D   shows that home bakers are proud people.

40 Extracts 1, 2 and 4 share the opinion that
    A   breadmaking is not as difficult as people think.
    B   only the best ingredients should be used in breadmaking.
    C   home baking can be a fascinating hobby.
    D   the mystery surrounding breadmaking should be respected.

PAPER 2   COMPOSITION   (2 hours)

*Write **two only** of the following composition exercises. Your answers must follow exactly the instructions given. Write in pen, not pencil. You are allowed to make alterations, but see that your work is clear and easy to read.*

1   Describe yourself as you imagine you will be in fifteen years' time. (About 350 words)

2   "The Olympic ideal is dead." Discuss. (About 350 words)

3   Write a story entitled "The Gambler". (About 350 words)

4   Write sets of instructions explaining *two* of the following, using about 150 words for each.

> how to make an omelette
> how to mend a bicycle puncture
> how to look after a dog while its owner is on holiday
> how to light a fire

5   Basing your answer on your reading of the prescribed text concerned, answer *one* of the following. (About 350 words)

GEORGE ELIOT: *Silas Marner*
What part does the Cass family play in the novel?

ROBERT GRAVES: *Goodbye To All That*
"The First World War was a tragic story of waste and futility."
How does *Goodbye To All That* illustrate this statement?

MARGARET DRABBLE: *The Millstone*
Rosamund describes herself as a "strange mixture of confidence and cowardice".
How are these two characteristics responsible for what happens to her?

PAPER 3   USE OF ENGLISH   (2 hours)

SECTION A

1   *Fill each of the numbered blanks in the following passage with* **one** *suitable word.*

From a close study of history you would never gain the impression that

human behaviour is dictated by intelligence, ... (1) less by

responsible morality. An observer from .... (2) planet, devoid

.... (3) instincts himself and unaware of the way in

.... (4) instincts, the aggressive instinct in .... (5),

operate among us, would be at a complete .... (6) to explain

history at .... (7). The phenomena of history do ....

(8) have reasonable causes. It is a mere commonplace .... (9) say

that they are caused by .... (10) common parlance so aptly

.... (11) "human nature". Unreasoning and unreasonable

human nature .... (12) two nations compete, even though

.... (13) economic necessity compels them to ....

(14) so. It induces two political parties, with amazingly similar programmes

.... (15) salvation, to fight .... (16) other bitterly. It impels   an   Alexander ....(17)   a   Napoleon   to   sacrifice

.... (18) of lives .... (19) an attempt to impose unity

.... (20) the world he knows.

2   *Finish each of the following sentences in such a way that it means exactly the same as the sentence printed before it.*

EXAMPLE: Immediately after his arrival, things went wrong.

ANSWER: No sooner *had he arrived than things went wrong.*

a)   It is said that he escaped to a neutral country.

He ....

b)   The truth only came out on the publication of the general's personal diaries.

Only when ....

c)   Oil was slowly coating the edge of the shore.

The edge of the shore ....

d)   In spite of the forecast it stayed fine.

Although rain ....

e)   We'd prefer you not to smoke.

We'd rather ....

f)   You really should be able to dress yourself by now!

It's high ....

g)   Provided your handwriting is legible the examiner will accept your answer.

So long as the examiner ....

3 *Fill each of the blanks with a suitable word or phrase.*

> EXAMPLE: Even if I had stood on a chair, *I wouldn't have been able to*
> *reach the light bulb.*

a) Serves him right. He .... better than to trust such
a shifty character.

b) I am not used to .... like that, you rude little boy!

c) The whole thing is pure fiction! You've .... up.

d) I'm afraid I can't, because I've run out of film. In ....
taking photographs here is forbidden.

e) I felt a gun in my back. A voice hissed: "Don't move ....
shoot."

f) .... gone to the dinner would have been very
rude.

g) Thank you .... custom. We are pleased to have
been of service.

h) Doctors say that the less one smokes .... one is
likely to live.

4 *For each of the sentences below, write a new sentence* **as similar as**
possible in meaning to the original sentence, *but using the word given.*
This word must **not be altered** *in any way.*

> EXAMPLE: His arrival was completely unexpected.
> **took**
>
> ANSWER: *His arrival took us completely by surprise.*

a) Don't pay any attention to what she says.
notice

....

b) He will have to accept your offer.
   option

   ....

c) Not many people attended the meeting.
   turnout

   ....

d) He has definitely agreed to accept the job.
   committed

   ....

e) The old lady's handbag had been stolen.
   robbed

   ....

f) There's an unpleasant odour of sweaty socks in here!
   smells

   ....

g) Is homework compulsory at that school?
   have

   ....

SECTION B

5 *Read the following passage, then answer the questions which follow it.*

Now at last the Collector's long day was over. A lamp was burning in his
study and in the glass of the bookcases he saw his own image, shadowy in
detail, wearing an already rather tattered morning coat, the face also in
shadow, anonymous, the face of a man like other men, who in a few years
would be lost to history, whose personality would be no more individual   5
than the shadowy reflection in the glass. "How alike we all are, really . . . .
There's so little difference between one man and another when one comes to
think of it."

        As he moved to turn out the lamp before going upstairs he thought how
normal everything still was here. It might have been any evening of the   10
years he had spent in Krishnapur. Only his ragged coat, his boots soiled
from digging graves, his poorly trimmed whiskers, and his exhausted
appearance would have given one to suspect that there was anything amiss.
That and the sound of gunfire from the compound.

On his way upstairs he passed Miriam in the hall and, without particularly   15
meaning to, he paused and put his arm around her. She was on her hands
and knees when this happened, searching the floor with a candle for some
pearls she had dropped when the string she was wearing had broken; in
spite of their increasingly ragged appearance it had become the habit for the
ladies to wear all the jewellery they possessed for safe-keeping. When the   20
Collector touched her she did not faint or seem offended; she returned the
pressure quite firmly and then sat back on her heels, brushing a lock of hair
out of her eyes with her knuckles because her hands were dirty. She looked
at him for a long time but did not say anything. After a while she went on
looking for her pearls and he went on his way upstairs. He did not know   25
what had made him do that. It had been discouragement more than anything.
He had been feeling the need for some kind of comfort . . . perhaps any kind
would have done . . . a good bottle of claret, for example, instead. Still, Mrs
Lang was a sensible woman and he did not think she would mind. "Funny
creatures, women, all the same," he mused. "One never knows, quite what   30
goes on in their minds."

Later, while he was drinking tea at the table in his bedroom with three
young officers a succession of musket balls came through the window,
attracted by the oil-lamp . . . one, two, three, and then a fourth, one after
another. The officers dived smartly under the table, leaving the Collector to   35
drink his tea alone. After a while they re-emerged smiling sheepishly,
deeply impressed by the Collector's sangfroid. Realising that he had forgotten
to sweeten his tea, the Collector dipped a teaspoon into the sugar-bowl. But
then he found that he was unable to keep the sugar on the spoon: as quickly
as he scooped it up, it danced off again. It was clear that he would never get   40
it from the sugar-bowl to his cup without scattering it over the table, so in
the end he was obliged to push the sugar away and drink his tea unsweetened.
Luckily, none of the officers had noticed.

That night, as soon as he closed his eyes, he found himself drawn down
into a sleep where shattering events raged back and forth over his unconscious   45
mind. Gradually, however, they receded and he fell into a more calm,
profound sleep . . . but not so profound that he could not hear, though from
afar, the heart-rending screams of Mrs Scott giving birth a few rooms away
on the next floor. Once, he suddenly started up in bed, thinking: "The poor
mite! What a world to be born into!" but perhaps that was merely part of a   50
long, sad, ineffably sad dream he had before dawn.

a)   In what way was the Collector's image "anonymous" (line 4)?

....

....

b) Apart from the Collector's physical appearance and condition, what else was "amiss" (line 13)?

....

....

c) How had Miriam come to drop her pearls?

....

....

d) Why might the ladies have looked rather strange wearing jewellery?

....

....

e) What does "that" (line 26) refer to?

....

....

f) What did the Collector think caused him to behave towards Miriam as he did?

....

....

g) How did he think she would feel about the incident?

....

....

⟫→

h) Explain the phrase "attracted by the oil-lamp" (line 34).

....

....

i) Explain fully the phrase "they re-emerged smiling sheepishly" (line 36).

....

....

j) What action of the Collector's demonstrated his "sangfroid" (line 37)?

....

....

k) What precisely did the officers fail to notice, and why was it lucky they did so?

....

....

l) What prevented the Collector from sleeping soundly that night?

....

....

m) Who or what was the "poor mite" (lines 49–50)?

....

....

n) Describe, in 60–80 words, the Collector's physical condition and appearance, and his state of mind.

....

....

....

....

....

....

....

....

....

....

....

PAPER 4 LISTENING COMPREHENSION
(about 30 minutes)

FIRST PART

For questions 1–10 tick whether each statement is true or false.

	True	False
1 Whitaker's Almanac is mainly a reference book about politicians.		
2 It is used for amusement as well as work.		
3 It is published in two volumes.		
4 It was first published 150 years ago.		
5 The book contains extracts from readers' letters.		
6 There have been four editors.		
7 Material for one edition is already being written before the previous one has been published.		
8 It is used by writers of fiction.		
9 The editor loses sleep on account of his job.		
10 Information is given only about the English-speaking world.		

SECOND PART

For questions 11 and 12 fill in the missing information in the spaces provided.

11   You wish to travel from Westbury to London on a Saturday morning using a cheap 'Awayday Return' ticket.

   (i)   Departure time from Westbury ....

   (ii) Cost of a ticket ....

12   You wish to travel from Westbury to London on a Sunday, using an ordinary single ticket on the 1707.

   (i)   arrival time in London ....

   (ii) changing at ....

   (iii) cost of a ticket ....

THIRD PART

*For questions 13 and 14 tick **one** of the boxes A, B, C or D. For question 15 tick the appropriate boxes i–vi.*

13   Pauline missed her flight because

   A   her visa had expired.

   B   she didn't have the right documents.

   C   it was foggy.

   D   she was at the wrong airport.

| A |
| B |
| C |
| D |

14   Where did Pauline finally fly from?

   A   Newcastle

   B   London

   C   Gatwick

   D   Luton

| A |
| B |
| C |
| D |

15 Indicate which of the following things caused Pauline problems.

i   unhelpful people ☐

ii   waiting for a visa in London ☐

iii bad weather ☐

iv   her friend in London wasn't at home ☐

v   she couldn't contact the airline by telephone ☐

vi   her travel agent misinformed her ☐

FOURTH PART

16 *Below are eight complaints and the names of five radio programmes. For each programme there is one complaint. Write the number of the complaint in the box beside the programme.*

Complaints

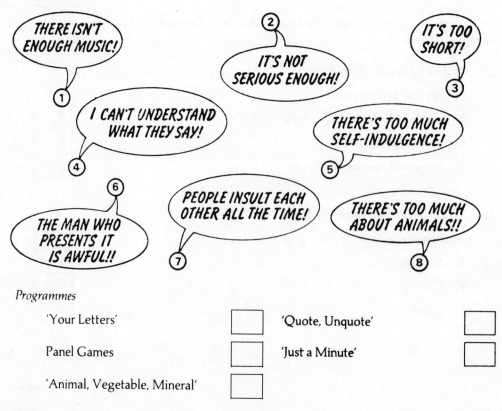

Programmes

'Your Letters' ☐   'Quote, Unquote' ☐

Panel Games ☐   'Just a Minute' ☐

'Animal, Vegetable, Mineral' ☐

PAPER 5   INTERVIEW   (15–20 minutes)

You will be asked to take part in a conversation with a group of other students or with your teacher. The conversation will be based on one particular topic area or theme, for example holidays, work, food.

Of course each interview will be different for each student or group of students, but a *typical* interview is described below.

★ At the start of the interview you will be asked to talk about one of the photographs among the Interview Exercises at the back of the book.

★ You will then be asked to discuss one of the passages at the back of the book. Your teacher may ask you to talk about its content, where you think it comes from, who the author or speaker is, whether you agree or disagree with it, and so on. You will *not* be asked to read the passage aloud, but you may quote parts of it to make your point.

★ You may then be asked to discuss for example an advertisement, a leaflet, extract from a newspaper etc. Your teacher will tell you which of the Interview Exercises to look at.

★ You may also be asked to take part in an activity with a group of other students or your teacher. Your teacher will tell you which section among the Interview Exercises you should look at.

Practice Test 5

PAPER 1   READING COMPREHENSION   (1 hour)

Answer all questions. Indicate your choice of answer in every case **on the separate answer sheet** *already given out, which should show your name and examination index number. Follow carefully the instructions about how to record your answers. Give* **one answer only** *to each question. Marks will not be deducted for wrong answers: your total score on this test will be the number of correct answers you give.*

SECTION A

In this section you must choose the word or phrase which best completes each sentence. **On your answer sheet** *indicate the letter A, B, C or D against the number of each item 1 to 25 for the word or phrase you choose.*

1   He always did well at school .... having his early education disrupted by illness.
     A on account of   B in spite of   C in addition to   D even though

2   He's determined to finish the job .... long it takes.
     A whatever   B whenever   C however   D no matter

3   The newspaper did not mention the .... of the damage caused by the fire.
     A range   B extent   C amount   D quantity

4   After a quick .... at the patient the doctor rang for an ambulance.
     A glance   B stare   C gaze   D glimpse

5   He was very taken .... by her aggressive attitude.
     A about   B aside   C apart   D aback

6   There is no evidence that any member of the Government is .... in the current scandals.
     A connected   B corrupted   C participated   D implicated

7   Your decision will .... a great strain on our friendship.
     A impose   B propose   C expose   D suppose

8   We could have provided him with a detached house but he .... asked
    for a small flat.
    A decidedly   B specifically   C strongly   D solely

9   This missile is designed so that once .... nothing can be done to
    retrieve it.
    A fired   B having fired   C they fired   D firing

10 I .... that you won't be inviting that awful woman to the meeting.
    A assume   B instruct   C entrust   D rely

11 He has put his car entirely at our .... for the holiday.
    A usage   B disposal   C pleasure   D disposition

12 His bank had never been .... of his change of address.
    A contacted   B notified   C acquainted   D communicated

13 The police were very .... in their examination of the building.
    A exhausting   B intense   C thorough   D concentrated

14 The roadworks made .... to the hotel from the main road difficult.
    A entrance   B approach   C access   D ways in

15 After he set fire to the library, the boy was .... from school.
    A expelled   B excluded   C exiled   D extracted

16 The museum wishes to .... an assistant curator for its fossil
    collection.
    A appoint   B commission   C authorise   D assign

17 They can't .... on a name for the baby.
    A conclude   B decide   C consent   D assent

18 They could find no .... of the missing car despite an extensive search.
    A clue   B remnant   C indication   D trace

19 I am never free on Tuesday evenings as I have a .... arrangement to
    go to the cinema with a friend.
    A long-standing   B long-lived   C long-range   D long-lasting

20 Having made his first film earlier this year, he is .... starring in a new
    musical.
    A actually   B recently   C currently   D lately

21 He was very quick to assert his authority .... the younger children.
    A on   B over   C to   D at

⟫→

22 I could stand the .... no longer and flung the door open.
    A expectation   B suspense   C foresight   D imagination

23 I'd rather you .... anything about the garden until the weather
    improves.
    A don't make   B didn't do   C don't do   D didn't make

24 Because of his poor health, it took him a long time to .... his bad cold.
    A throw off   B throw away   C throw down   D throw over

25 She pointed out that her wages .... no relation to the amount of work
    she did.
    A held   B yielded   C offered   D bore

SECTION B

*In this section you will find after each of the passages a number of questions or
unfinished statements about the passage, each with four suggested answers or ways of
finishing. You must choose the one which you think fits best according to the passage.*
On your answer sheet, *indicate the letter A, B, C or D against the number of each
item 26 to 40 for the answer you choose. Give* **one answer only** *to each question.
Read each passage right through before choosing your answers.*

FIRST PASSAGE

Naturally the young are more inclined to novelty than their elders and it is in
their speech, as it always was, that most of the verbal changes originate. But
listening critically to their talk I hear hardly any new words. It is all a matter of
using old words in a new way and then copying each other, for much as they
wish to speak differently from their parents, they want even more to speak like
people of their own age. A new usage once took time to spread, but now a pop
star can flash it across the world in hours.
    Of course it is not only the young who like to use the latest in-word. While
they are describing their idols as *smashing, great, fab* or *cosmic,* their parents and
the more discriminating of the younger set are also groping for words of praise
that are at once apt and fashionable. However, their choice of *splendid,
brilliant, fantastic* and so on will in turn be slightly dimmed by over-use and
need replacement.
    Magic is a theme that has regularly supplied words of praise (and the
choice must betray something in our nature). *Charming, entrancing* and *enchanting*
are all based on it. So also is *marvellous,* which has been used so much that some
of its magic has faded while among teenagers *wizard* had a great run. Another of
this group, though you might not think it, is *glamorous,* which was all the rage
in the great days of Hollywood. *Glamour* was a Scottish dialect form of
"grammar" or "grammarye", which itself was an old word for *enchantment.*

(*Grammar* means the study of words, and words have always been at the heart of magic.) The change from "r" to "l" may have come about through the association with words like *gleaming* and *glittering*.

On the whole, when a new word takes over the old ones remain, weakened but still in use, so that the total stock increases all the time. But some that start only as slang and never rise above that class can disappear completely. "Did you really say *ripping* when you were young?" my granddaughter asked me, rather like asking if I ever wore a suit of armour. Of course I did and it was no sillier than *smashing*, which some of her contemporaries are still saying.

26 What do young people like to do in their speech?
   A invent words that older people cannot understand
   B use words invented by pop stars
   C give words new meanings to mislead their parents
   D copy the speech of their contemporaries

27 Words of praise keep changing because
   A they lose their freshness.
   B there are more words available in this area.
   C young people are becoming more discriminating.
   D older people try to avoid the in-words of the young.

28 The fact that magic is a frequent source of words of praise suggests that people
   A lack linguistic originality.
   B have always been interested in magic.
   C are becoming more superstitious.
   D are interested in magic when young.

29 Which of these words does not have an association with magic?
   A marvellous
   B grammar
   C gleaming
   D wizard

30 To the author's granddaughter the word *ripping*
   A seems strange and old-fashioned.
   B has a clearer meaning than it does for the author.
   C is unacceptable because it is slang.
   D means much the same as *smashing*.

SECOND PASSAGE

Chris Baildon, tall and lean, was in his early thirties, and the end-product of an old decayed island family.

Chris shared the too large house with his father, an arthritic and difficult man, and a wasp-tongued aunt, whose complaints ended only when she slept.

The father and his sister, Chris's Aunt Agatha, engaged in shrill-voiced arguments over nothing. The continuous exchanges further confused their foolish wits, and yet held off an unendurable loneliness. They held a common grievance against Chris, openly holding him to blame for their miserable existence. He should long ago have lifted them from poverty, for had they not sacrificed everything to send him to England and Oxford University?

Driven by creditors or pressing desires, earlier Baildons had long ago cheaply disposed of valuable properties. Brother and sister never ceased to remind each other of the depressing fact that their ancestors had wasted their inheritance. This, in fact, was their only other point of agreement.

A few years earlier Agatha had announced that she intended doing something about repairing the family fortunes. The many empty rooms could be rented to selected guests. She would establish, not a boarding-house, but a home for ladies and gentlemen, and make a tidy profit. She threw herself into the venture with a noisy fury. Old furniture was polished; rugs and carpets were beaten, floors painted, long-stored mattresses, pillows and bed-linen aired and sweetened in the sun. The huge kitchen was attacked.

Agatha, with a fine air of defiance, took the copy for a modest advertisement to the press. Two guests were lured by the promise of beautiful gourmet meals, a home atmosphere in an historic mansion, the company of well-brought-up ladies and gentlemen. The two, one a bank-clerk and the other a maiden lady employed in a bookshop, arrived simultaneously, whereupon Agatha condescended to show them to their rooms, and promptly forgot about them. There was no hot water. Dinnertime found Baildon and Agatha sharing half a cold chicken and a few boiled potatoes in the dining-room's gloomy vastness.

When the guests came timidly to inquire about the dining hours, and to point out that there were no sheets on the beds, no water in the pitchers, no towels on their racks, Agatha reminded them that the Baildons were not inn-keepers, and then treated them to an account of the family's past glories.

31 The quarrels of the father and aunt
    A were due to their sheer love of argument.
    B caused Chris great sadness.
    C made them forget their unhappy life.
    D arose from common ill-health.

32 His father and aunt blamed Chris for
    A not succeeding at Oxford University.
    B neglecting the family property.
    C taking no interest in family history.
    D not restoring their prosperity.

33 What do we learn about the Baildons' ancestors?
   A They had been treated unfairly.
   B They had always been poor.
   C They were bad managers.
   D They didn't maintain their house properly.

34 Agatha hoped to attract guests who
   A were of the right social class.
   B were prepared to help in the house.
   C got on well with each other.
   D would not be very demanding.

35 Agatha's venture was unlikely to succeed because
   A the house was too isolated.
   B she had no interest in her guests.
   C she lacked experience of domestic work.
   D the guests did not like the food.

THIRD PASSAGE

Extract 1

It was going to be an epic experience. Everybody assured me of it. The train journey, they said, south from Fort William in Scotland, is the most scenic, the most awe-inspiring, the most breathtaking in Britain. The Highlands, Glencoe, the Moor of Rannoch, Loch Lomond, all, all this would be mine, and by the time I reached the whisky warehouses of Dumbarton I should be ready to retire to my sleeper worn out with wonder and weighed down by British Rail cuisine.

In a state of high expectation, I boarded the 18.22 at Fort William, found a quiet window-seat affording unimpeded panoramic views, resolutely closed my book and settled back. I would adjourn to the dining car, I mused, on the Moor of Rannoch and take coffee as we skirted Loch Lomond.

Extract 2

'Stanley,' said a voice behind me, 'what did you do with the thermos flask?'
'It's in the carrier bag next to the cheese biscuits. I put it in fresh this morning.'
'No you never, Stanley. We finished the cheese biscuits last night on the coach. You know we did, because you put your banana skin and wrappers in the box and threw it in that litter basket at Glenfinnan.'
'Maybe it's in the string bag. Have you looked in the string bag?'
'Strewth, Stanley, what did you go and put it in there for? Now see what you've gone and done. You've squashed the pork pie, shoving it in like that. Why don't you ever think, Stanley?'

>>>→

Extract 3

I looked out of the window. The sun shone. The rivers splashed over rocks coloured every shade of the rainbow. A deer dashed across a clearing into a thicket, and the backdrop of sun-capped mountains could have been freshly cut out of marzipan.

'What time will you be serving dinner?' I asked the ticket inspector. He looked at me strangely.

'They'll put on a microbuffet with coffee and sandwiches at Rannoch as far as Dumbarton,' he said.

'You mean there's no dining car or even a bar?' I said incredulously.

'Not on this line; it doesn't pay. You should have gone to Inverness if you wanted a proper meal.'

Extract 4

The guard brought me a cup of tea for consolation, and when we got to Glasgow I retired for the night, worn out with wonder and weighed down with potato crisps. At 7 a.m. we reached Stafford. At 9 a.m. we were still there because our engine had broken down. At 10 a.m. the spare engine arrived. Thanks to further engine failure, we were able to spend a full half-hour sightseeing at Nuneaton Station, and I have never seen such awe manifest on the faces of a group of travellers as that inspired by the first sight of the backyards of Mornington Crescent, heralding the misty lunchtime magnificence of Euston Station.

36   Which extract makes the place name(s) mentioned sound romantic?
    A extract 1   B extract 2   C extract 3   D extract 4

37   In which extract does the writer express complete contentment?
    A extract 1   B extract 2   C extract 3   D extract 4

38   Which extract makes ironic reference to the language of another extract?
    A extract 1   B extract 2   C extract 3   D extract 4

39   Which sentence suggests that the speaker is rather uneducated?
    A   No you never, Stanley.
    B   Not on this line; it doesn't pay.
    C   You mean there's no dining car?
    D   Why don't you ever think, Stanley?

40   Who is Stanley?
    A   the writer
    B   the microbuffet attendant
    C   a passenger unknown to the writer
    D   the ticket inspector

PAPER 2   COMPOSITION   (2 hours)

*Write **two only** of the following composition exercises. Your answers must follow exactly the instructions given. Write in pen, not pencil. You are allowed to make alterations, but make sure that your work is clear and easy to read.*

1   Describe an interesting or eccentric family that you know. (About 350 words)

2   "Children today are given too much freedom." How true do you think this is? (About 350 words)

3   Write a story entitled "The Robbery". (About 350 words)

4   Below is a diagram of a new telephone device. How would you explain its advantages for an elderly person living alone? (About 300 words)

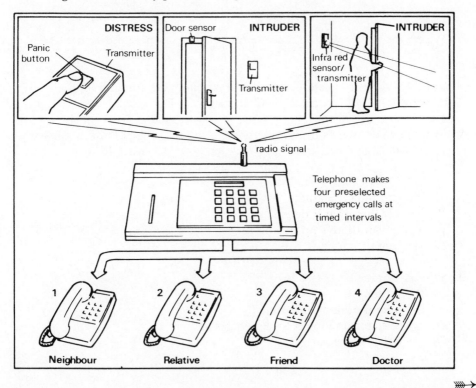

5   Basing your answer on your reading of the prescribed text concerned,
    answer *one* of the following. (About 350 words)

    GEORGE ELIOT: *Silas Marner*
    Describe the part played by gold in *Silas Marner*.

    PATRICIA HIGHSMITH: *The Talented Mr Ripley*
    Do you agree that because we know who committed the murders there is no
    suspense or excitement in this novel?

    JOHN ARDEN: *Serjeant Musgrave's Dance*
    "Common sense triumphs at the end of *Serjeant Musgrave's Dance*." How
    true do you find this?

PAPER 3   USE OF ENGLISH   (2 hours)

SECTION A

1   *Fill each of the numbered blanks in the following passage with* **one** *suitable word.*

It has been established beyond a shadow of doubt that readers in general waste a great deal of time and effort. Why is this .... (1)? Why is it that the poorest readers by .... (2) standard are often the ablest .... (3) people? Why is it that the majority of students have very .... (4) idea of how to tackle .... (5) reading? Why is it that a high .... (6) of readers – not excluding those .... (7) professional work involves a lot of reading – use a technique that is .... (8) more advanced than .... (9) they were children?

Or why .... (10) there people – to take an extreme but illuminating .... (11) – who in conversation and discussion .... (12) sustain a difficult argument with ease and .... (13) who as readers assimilate only factual information, and .... (14) that with difficulty, so that worthwhile books are virtually .... (15) them? In our opinion, reading presents technical .... (16) of communication that dispose the .... (17) to use inappropriate methods of assimilation; this,

[95]

and only .... (18), can provide an adequate .... (19)

of why readers .... (20) a class are so inefficient.

2 Finish each of the following sentences in such a way that it means exactly the same as the sentence printed before it.

EXAMPLE: Immediately after his arrival, things went wrong.

ANSWER: No sooner *had he arrived than things went wrong.*

a) Without his help we would all have died.

If it ....

b) He forgot about the gun until he got home.

Not until ....

c) May I borrow your pen?

Would you mind ....

d) "I'd take a taxi if I were you," said Peter.

Peter suggested ....

e) My boyfriend is very short-tempered.

My boyfriend loses ....

f) You can use it as long as you like, and it won't wear out.

No matter ....

g) If the work is finished by lunchtime you can go home.

Get ....

h) Although Judy was severely disabled she participated in many sports.

Despite her ....

3   *Fill each of the blanks with a suitable word or phrase.*

EXAMPLE: Even if I had stood on a chair, *I wouldn't have been able to* reach the light bulb.

a)   You'll have to get .... on the left, if you take your car to England.

b)   I wish I .... up smoking.

c)   It's not a perfect fit, but it will do for .... being.

d)   The trains are very infrequent. You'd .... off taking a bus.

e)   She was said .... her third novel before she was twenty.

f)   We must leave by four o'clock because it .... at least an hour to get there.

4   *For each of the sentences below, write a new sentence* **as similar as possible in meaning to the original sentence**, *but using the word given. This word must* **not** *be altered in any way.*

EXAMPLE: Not many people attended the meeting.
    turnout

ANSWER: *There was a poor turnout for the meeting.*

a)   It is certain that the new cuts will worry the staff.
    bound

    ....

b)   John is very dependable.
    let

    ....

c)   They accused me of causing the accident.
    blame

    ....

d)   They are unlikely to come.
    doubtful

    ....

e) His favourite breakfast is porridge and kippers.
   what

   ....

f) After the scandal he was asked to resign.
   hand

   ....

g) That's got nothing to do with you.
   business

   ....

h) I'd never been to Rome before.
   visiting

   ....

SECTION B

5 *Read the following passage, then answer the questions which follow it.*

Now I have had, at one time or another, a fair amount of experience in trying
to get frightened, irritated or just plain stupid animals to feed from a bottle,
and I thought that I knew most of the tricks. The wildcat kitten I had
proceeded to show me that, as far as it was concerned, I was a mere tyro at
the game. It was so lithe, quick and strong for its size that after half an hour   5
of struggling etc. I felt a total failure. I was covered in milk and blood and
thoroughly exhausted, whereas the kitten regarded me with blazing eyes
and seemed quite ready to continue the fight for the next three days if
necessary. The thing that really irritated me was that the kitten had – as I
knew to my cost – very well developed teeth, and there seemed no reason   10
why it should not eat and drink of its own accord, but, in this stubborn
mood, I knew that it was capable of quite literally starving itself to death.
        I decided to try another tack. Perhaps it would eat if it had a companion
to show it how. I chose a fat, placid female tabby cat and carried it back to
the garage. Now most wild animals have a very strong sense of territory. In   15
the wild state, they have their own particular bit of forest or grassland which
they consider their own preserve, and which they will defend against any
other member of their own species that tries to enter it. When you put wild
animals into cages, cages become, as far as they are concerned, their
territory. So if you introduce another animal into the same cage, the first   20
inmate will in all probability defend it vigorously, and you may easily have a
fight to the death on your hands. So you generally have to employ low
cunning. Suppose, for example, you have a large vigorous creature and you

get a second animal of the same species, and you want to confine them together. The best thing to do is to build an entirely new cage, and into this 25 you introduce the weaker of the two animals. When it has settled down, you then put the stronger one in with it. The stronger one will, of course, still remain the dominant animal, but as far as he is concerned he has been introduced into someone else's territory, and this takes the edge off his potential viciousness. 30

In this case I was sure that the baby wildcat was quite capable of killing the domestic kitten, if I introduced the kitten to it instead of the other way round. So, once the tabby had settled down, I seized the wildcat and pushed it, snarling and raving, into the cage, and stood back to see what would happen. The tabby was delighted. It came forward to the angry intruder and 35 started to rub itself against its neck, purring loudly. The wildcat, taken aback by its greeting, merely spat rather rudely and retreated into a corner. I covered the front of the cage with a piece of sacking and left them to settle down.

That evening, when I lifted the sacking, I found them lying side by side, 40 and the wildcat, instead of spitting at me as it had done up until now, contented itself with merely lifting its lips in a warning manner. I carefully inserted a large bowl of milk into the cage, and a plate containing the finely chopped meat and raw egg, which I wanted the wildcat to eat. This was the crucial test. 45

The tabby, purring like an ancient outboard engine, flung itself at the bowl of milk, took a long drink and then settled down to the meat and egg. To begin with the wildcat took no interest at all, lying there with half-closed eyes. But eventually the noise the tabby was making over the egg and meat – it was a rather messy feeder – attracted its attention. It rose cautiously 50 and approached the plate while I held my breath. Delicately it sniffed round the edge of the plate, while the tabby lifted a face that was dripping with raw egg and gave a mew of encouragement, slightly muffled by the portion of meat it had in its mouth. The wildcat stood pondering for a moment and then, to my delight, sank down by the plate and started to eat. In spite of the 55 fact that it must have been extremely hungry, it ate daintily, lapping a little raw egg, and then picking up a morsel of meat which it chewed thoroughly before swallowing. I knew my battle with the wildcat was won.

a) Explain what the writer means by the phrase "a mere tyro at the game" (lines 4–5).

    ....

    ....

b) What evidence is there of the writer's failure (line 6)?

    ....

....

....

c) Explain in your own words what "really irritated" the writer (line 9).

....

....

d) What reason did the wildcat have for starving itself?

....

e) What is meant by the phrase "sense of territory" (line 15)?

....

f) How does this sense affect the behaviour of animals both in the wild and in captivity?

....

....

g) Explain the phrase "low cunning" as it is used in lines 22–23.

....

h) How does the writer suggest you should go about confining a strong animal with a weaker one?

....

....

i) Explain the phrase "potential viciousness" as it is used in line 30.

....

j) How does the wildcat behave towards the writer and towards the tabby kitten when first introduced into the cage? What words suggest that it had calmed down by the evening?

....

....

....

k) In what way was the test "crucial" (line 45)?

....

l) What is implied about ancient outboard engines (line 46)?

....

m) Why did the writer hold his breath (line 51)?

....

n) Explain in your words what was "dainty" about the wildcat's method of eating.

....

....

o) In a paragraph of about 60-80 words, summarise the steps the writer had to take in order to get the wildcat to eat.

....

....

....

....

....

....

....

....

....

....

....

PAPER 4   LISTENING COMPREHENSION
(about 30 minutes)

FIRST PART

Fill in the information you hear about the man and woman in the boxes below. Sentences are not necessary.

1

	Man	*Woman*
JOB		
LENGTH OF TIME IN THIS JOB		
TOWN/CITY WHERE HE/SHE WORKS		
TRANSPORT TO AND FROM WORK		
NUMBER OF CHILDREN		

SECOND PART

*For questions 2–5 tick **one** of the boxes A, B, C or D.*

2   What has affected the quality of crops in the past?

   A   poor soil

   B   fungi

   C   climate

   D   poor harvests

A
B ✗
C
D

3   How can the farmer improve his product?

   A   by better handling of the crops

   B   by better packing of the crops

   C   by better planting of the crops

   D   by better marketing of the crops

A ✗
B ✗
C
D

4   What is the main aim of the company?

   A   to reduce wastage

   B   to make a profit

   C   to increase exports

   D   to increase harvests

A	✓
B	
C	✓
D	

5   What will Jamaica do in the immediate future?

   A   concentrate on the UK market

   B   look to worldwide markets

   C   develop European markets

   D   turn to the American markets

A	
B	✗
C	
D	

THIRD PART

For questions 6–13 tick whether you think the statements are true or false.

		True	False
6	150,000 French people have no electricity.		
7	Some people are waiting on house rooftops to be rescued.		
8	The forecast says the weather is going to improve soon.		
9	More people are beginning to watch Rise and Shine TV.		
10	Sonia Sefton and Nancy Morris have become sports reporters.		
11	Katherine Vickers had never worked for Rise and Shine before.		
12	The new Rise and Shine programmes will be more lively.		
13	Four TV directors were dismissed.		

FOURTH PART

For questions 14–16 tick **one** *of the boxes A, B, C or D.*

14   According to the speaker, the landlords

    A will only do major repairs.

    B say that repairs aren't their responsibility.

    C demand extra rent for doing repairs.

    D ignore requests for repairs.

A
B
C
D

15   Why don't the tenants complain to the landlords?

    A They never see the landlords.

    B They're afraid their rent will be increased.

    C They know they couldn't find anywhere else.

    D They're used to living in bad conditions.

A
B
C
D

16   What word best describes the woman's attitude?

    A angry

    B diffident

    C shocked

    D resigned

A
B
C
D

PAPER 5   INTERVIEW   (15–20 minutes)

You will be asked to take part in a conversation with a group of other students or with your teacher. The conversation will be based on one particular topic area or theme, for example holidays, work, food.

Of course each interview will be different for each student or group of students, but a *typical* interview is described below.

★ At the start of the interview you will be asked to talk about one of the photographs among the Interview Exercises at the back of the book.

★ You will then be asked to discuss one of the passages at the back of the book. Your teacher may ask you to talk about its content, where you think it comes from, who the author or speaker is, whether you agree or disagree with it, and so on. You will *not* be asked to read the passage aloud, but you may quote parts of it to make your point.

★ You may then be asked to discuss for example an advertisement, a leaflet, extract from a newspaper etc. Your teacher will tell you which of the Interview Exercises to look at.

★ You may also be asked to take part in an activity with a group of other students or your teacher. Your teacher will tell you which section among the Interview Exercises you should look at.

Interview Exercises

WEAPONS, TERRORISM AND VIOLENCE

1

2 Even dressed in civilian clothes, he looked very much a soldier. He was well over six feet tall, erect, rather stiff in carriage, and abrupt in speech and manner. He was a gallant figure, and you could see that his war experiences, including a long term of imprisonment and a dramatic escape, had not daunted his fighting spirit.

3 The 20 men and women still aboard the hijacked airliner were described over the telephone last night by our correspondent as being very brave. At least two other passengers are known to have been killed after delays in getting together a negotiating team to deal with the hijackers, who are demanding the release of 50 prisoners held by their enemies.

4 A man appeared in court yesterday charged with the assault and robbery of three elderly women in separate incidents in February and March this year. In each case, the man obtained entry to the house by pretending to be a specialist checking for damp. As soon as he was in the house, he rendered the woman unconscious by hitting her on the head, tying her hands and feet and gagging her. He then made off with whatever valuables and money he could find.

5

Royal Ordnance Small Arms Division is part of an independent company based at Enfield Lock, Middlesex. We enjoy an international reputation as a manufacturer of high quality engineering products, and equally a historic and proud record as a good responsible employer in the local community. As part of its continuing programme of expansion, we require the following personnel:

SKILLED CRAFTSMEN

Applicants for craftsman posts should have served a recognised apprenticeship, and have experience in one or more of the following skills—turning, milling, grinding.
There are vacancies for craftsmen to be trained in CNC and Special Purpose Machine Setting, and in the setting of conventional machine tools.
In addition, there are vacancies in both the toolroom and skilled production areas.
Attractive rates of pay are offered to successful applicants and there is a contributory pension scheme. Annual holiday allowance is 24 $\frac{1}{2}$ days per annum, from 1st February, 1986.
For an application form please write to the Personnel Officer, Royal Ordnance Small Arms Division, Ordnance Road, Enfield Lock, Middlesex, EN3 6JL, or telephone Lea Valley 763333, ext 3933.

NON-SKILLED WORKERS

Vacancies exist in the following grades:—
PRODUCTION OPERATORS
EXAMINERS
STOREKEEPERS
Applicants for these posts should ideally have experience of working in a light engineering environment, but training will be given to non-experienced candidates if selected.

SKILLED INSPECTORS

Applicants for these vacancies should have served a recognised apprenticeship and have a knowledge of modern inspection methods to British Standards, and will preferably have experience of co-ordinate measuring machines and electronic measuring devices. The ability to perform simple statistical calculations is essential.

Royal Ordnance plc is an Equal Opportunities Employer

ROYAL**ORDNANCE**

Defence systems sub-systems and components

6 The examiner will ask you to give your views on the following statement: "No government should give in to terrorism". You will be given a particular theme or themes to concentrate on.

FOOD AND DIET

8 More trucks of food reached the drought-stricken camps in central Africa today where thousands have died over the past few months. In this region, where it hasn't rained for three years, there is little chance of anything growing in the near future. These people will therefore be dependent on outside aid for some time to come.

9 When I go to the supermarket, I now scan the shelves for additive-free food, having recently discovered that one of my children is allergic to certain artificial colours. It's getting easier to find food without additives and more and more information is given on the labels. However, some foods still consist almost entirely of artificial ingredients and the worst thing about it is that these are mainly the kind of things that children like.

10 Well-balanced diets are vital in the formation and repair of body tissues, and for the production of heat and energy. Certain necessary chemical elements and complex groupings must be provided from which the body can make all it needs. The essential constituents are proteins, fats, carbohydrates, vitamins and minerals. The energy value of food is expressed in calories.

11

For just one day let him eat more than you.

Every day 40,000 children die because they don't have enough to eat.

Yet there is more than enough food in the world to go round. The trouble is, it doesn't.

Now is the time for you to do something positive about the situation. Join Oxfam's second Hungry for Change Fast.

In last year's Fast more than 50,000 people showed their concern for the starving, and demonstrated this concern to the government, by going without food.

This year put yourself on the line and join them. Even if it's only for one missed meal it's your commitment that's important.

Show you're hungry for change. Join the Fast. Just one day of your life could make all the difference to someone else.

┌─ ─ ─ ─ **I SUPPORT OXFAM'S SECOND HUNGRY FOR CHANGE FAST** ─ ─ ─ ─ ┐

☐ I'll fast. Please forward my name to my nearest Oxfam organiser. ☐ I'm not able to fast, but send me details of the Hungry for Change campaign. I enclose a donation of £_____

Name_____ Address_____

_____ Postcode_____ **OXFAM**

Send to: Oxfam, FREEPOST, Oxford OX2 7BR.
TO GET FAST DETAILS FAST, CONTACT YOUR AREA OXFAM ORGANISER THROUGH YOUR LOCAL PHONE DIRECTORY.

Oxfam works with poor people in their struggle against hunger, disease, exploitation and poverty in Africa, Asia, Latin-America and the Middle East through relief, development, research and public education.

12 The examiner will ask you to speak either for or against the following motion: "Every country should take steps to control the growth of its population".

 You may like to think about the following points when preparing your speech:
– financial incentives/disincentives
– effects of over-population
– aspects of personal freedom
– cultural considerations
– need to increase the population of some countries

LEISURE

13

14 I very seldom enter an English pub that has TV, popular music or video games, or is crowded. I prefer quiet little pubs where you can hear yourself. And of course where you are welcome. I hate it when it's so noisy that you have to pretend to listen and understand. I feel exactly as if I were a dog, barking at a familiar noise.

15   People's leisure time is ever increasing. For those in employment, the working week is gradually getting shorter and holidays are getting longer. Unemployment gives the jobless unlimited amounts of time to pursue leisure activities. However, facilities for leisure pursuits provided by society tend to cost more than the unemployed can afford and time can hang heavily on their hands.

16   These two saxophonists go together so well that you would never guess that they are of very different generations. Not that either Whittle (age 60) or Barnes (age 26) seems to be making any special effort to fit in with the other – it's just that they both play naturally in the timeless, central jazz idiom known as "mainstream". Each has a distinct musical personality. Together they make the kind of music you might hear on a particularly good night in one of London's jazz rooms, although slightly more succinct.

17

OCTOBER

THE KILLING FIELDS
Winner of three Oscars and eight British Academy Awards, a horrifying and true story of two men caught up in the terrors of the Cambodian war, one determined to tell the truth whatever the cost, the other whose integrity very nearly cost him his life. Both would never forget what they experienced in that beautiful war-torn country.

MORONS FROM OUTER SPACE

A delightful, totally daft film from TV's top funny men, Griff Rhys Jones and Mel Smith. Three complete idiots from beyond the galaxies crash-land their spaceship on the M1; governments and scientists eager to interrogate these humanoid aliens become completely frustrated with their lack of – well – anything!

COMING SOON

A PASSAGE TO INDIA
India – a land of spell-binding mystery. Under the stuffed-shirt rule of the British Raj, two English women attempt to discover the true India – with disastrous results. A film which won two Oscars, directed by David Lean, who brought us *Dr. Zhivago* and *Lawrence of Arabia*.

AMADEUS
The film of 1985 which swept the board at the Oscars ceremony, winning 8 awards in all including Best Picture, Best Director and Best Actor. Based on the masterpiece by Peter Shaffer, it tells the fascinating, horrifying and blackly comic story of the rivalry between the composer of the greatest music ever written and the man who worshipped, envied and hated him.

18   The examiner will ask you to talk about a special study or leisure
interest of your own.

ARCHITECTURE, ART AND LITERATURE

19

20   The whole history of painting is like this. First those who invent, then those who dilute, who produce something of lower intensity, some flabbier variant. Then those who do more or less good work in the accepted style of the period. Finally the art-phoneys or charlatans, the starters of crazes. Any one of these may be the genuine inventor of the next phase.

21   Well of course you have to realise that until 1968 when my first book came out, as far as the public were concerned I was nonexistent. In fact to myself I was almost nonexistent anyway so I never really moved in that world, as you might say. But in a different sense, I've always been liberated; at least I've felt myself to be liberated, and this comes out in my writing, I think.

22   The earliest permanent buildings, dating from about 4,000 BC in Egypt, reflect the grandeur of the ruling classes and their systems of worship. Progressive changes tended to embrace more varied and specialised structures to suit the needs of a greater portion of the population. From earliest times until the mid-nineteenth century all permanent building was governed by three structural principles.

23

New from *YALE*

Yale University Press
13 Bedford Square · London WC1B 3JF

Jesus through the Centuries
His Place in the History of Culture
Jaroslav Pelikan
This important book by a noted historian and theologian examines the impact of Jesus on the cultural, political, social, and economic history of the last two millennia. Studying the images of Jesus cherished by successive ages — from rabbi in the first century to universal man in the Renaissance to liberator in the nineteenth and twentieth centuries — Pelikan suggests that the way Jesus was depicted at a particular time in history is an essential key to understanding that age. *12 colour plates* **£16.95**

Cities and People
A Social and Architectural History
Mark Girouard
A delightful tour of the great cities of the world by the author of the best-selling *Life in the English Country House.* Focusing on such cities as London, Paris, New York, Venice, Los Angeles, and Constantinople at crucial periods in their history, Girouard discusses their architecture, their design, and the people who lived in them, making this book both a significant piece of social history and an irresistible delight.
200 b & w illus. + 120 colour plates **£16.95**

The Political Mythology of Apartheid
Leonard Thompson
This exciting and masterful work by a leading historian examines the causes and effects of political mythology, focusing on South Africa as a test case. Drawing on a wide range of material to explain the mythology behind Afrikaner racism, Thompson's book is an invaluable aid to understanding the background to the present situation in South Africa, while alerting historians and politicians to the prevalence of political mythologies throughout the modern world.
Illus. **£22.50**

24 The examiner will ask you to give a short talk describing an important painting or novel from your own country. You should also compare the subject matter and the style with a painting or novel from another country.

25

THE COUNTRYSIDE AND THE ENVIRONMENT

26

27 The west of Ireland is green and soft. There are hayfields, but much of the countryside is uncultivated. The roads wind across a wide, open landscape, passing here and there great stacks of peat waiting to dry out and be taken to the cottages for winter fuel. Above are the hillsides where the peat is dug, shining black and wet.

28 Sheep can be reared on many lands unfit for arable agriculture, and their use in rotation on arable land also helps to maintain its fertility. They do well in most temperate regions, especially on hilly land. Breeds are specialised either for wool or flesh production. Domesticated sheep are derived from wild species native to the drier uplands of central Asia.

29 The trend over recent years has been for farmers to make their fields bigger and bigger, destroying hedgerows, footpaths, natural habitats and wooded areas in the process. As a consequence, a lot of wild flowers, animals, birds and insects found in our countryside fifty years ago have disappeared in the name of agricultural production.

30

GREAT PLACES TO STAY
NEW PEOPLE TO MEET

The YHA is a worldwide club that offers you the chance to get away and combine adventure and leisure to the exact mix that suits you. Get up and go — discover this country and others at prices which don't cost the earth.

With a network of 260 hostels all over England and Wales, the YHA offers a superb range of places to stay. Fancy catching a night in a ghostly Norman castle, an elegant Georgian mansion or somewhere a stone's throw from a sandy beach? They're all part of the YHA — whether you want to visit the city or countryside, there's usually a hostel close by. And the prices are remarkable. . . a night's stay costs from around £3.00.

All ages are welcome at YHA. Whether you're getting around with a group or going it alone, YHA hostels make a great base for your holiday. Stay in one and find out where the action is. Hostels buzz with social activity. They make super centres for groups too, organising anything from school trips to fell rambles.

If it's a week or just a weekend you're planning, though, there's one thing all our hostels have in common — the warmest welcome for you.

Most provide tempting low cost meals or snacks. But if you'd rather make something tasty yourself there's always a self catering kitchen. You sleep in bunk-bedded rooms or dormitories with showers and central heating in all but the most isolated country hostels, where a chat with new found friends around a log fire in the common room and breath-taking surroundings are the main attractions.

31

The examiner will ask you to speak either for or against the following motion: "Pollution is a necessary evil". You may like to think about the following points when preparing your speech:
- (unforeseen) damage to the environment
- the need for power, chemicals etc. in a modern society
- harmful media scares versus "cover-ups"
- damage to health
- alternatives to pollution-creating processes (i.e. lead-free petrol)

OPTIONAL READING

GEORGE ELIOT: *Silas Marner*

32

33 It was impossible for the neighbours to doubt that Marner was telling the truth, not because they were capable of arguing at once from the nature of his statements to the absence of any motive for making them falsely, but because, as Mr Macey observed, "Folks as had the devil to back 'em were not likely to be so mushed" as poor Silas was.

34 As I say, Mr Have-your-own-way is the best husband, and the only one I'd ever promise to obey. I know it isn't pleasant, when you've been used to living in a big way, and managing hogshead and all that, to go and put your nose in by somebody else's fireside, or to sit down by yourself to a scrag or a knuckle; but, thank God! my father's a sober man and likely to live.

35 This excessive rumination and self-questioning is perhaps a morbid habit inevitable to a mind of much moral sensibility when shut out from its due share of outward activity and of practical claims on its affections – inevitable to a noblehearted, childless woman, when her lot is narrow. "I can do so little – have I done it all well?" is the perpetually recurring thought.

36 The examiner will ask you to discuss one or more of the following topics:
1 The importance of any one or two characters from the text.
2 The situation of any one or more characters, in a "What could he/she have done?" context.
3 Reasons for the text's popularity.
4 Insights into the life of the time portrayed.
5 Present-day relevance of the text's themes and attitudes.
6 Stage or film versions of the text.

MARGARET DRABBLE: *The Millstone*

37

38   And he looked at me, oblique, slanted, his words full of implications yet so mild and harmless, so much on my side, so little against me, so little a threat that I felt weak with relief. I thought, looking at him, that he was almost very handsome; with a little more weight he might have been a handsome man.

39   No, no, I couldn't possibly do that, they both said at once, their voices hardening from personal timidity and embarrassment into the weight of authority. They had that whole building behind them, they knew, and I had nothing behind me at all except my intention.

40   For five minutes or so, I almost hoped that she might die, and thus relieve me of the corruption and the fatality of love. Ben Jonson said of his dead child, my sin was too much hope of thee, loved boy. We too easily take what the poets write as figures of speech, as pretty images, as strings of *bon mots*. Sometimes perhaps they speak the truth.

41   The examiner will ask you to discuss one or more of the following topics:
1 The importance of any one or two characters from the text.
2 The situation of any one or more characters, in a "What could he/she have done?" context.
3 Reasons for the text's popularity.
4 Insights into the life of the time portrayed.
5 Present-day relevance of the text's themes and attitudes.
6 Stage or film versions of the text.

Acknowledgements

The University of Cambridge Local Examinations Syndicate and the publishers are grateful to the following for permission to reproduce texts and illustrations. It has not been possible to identify sources of all the material used and in such cases the publishers would welcome information from copyright owners.

The estate of Barbara Pym for the extract on p.6 from *Excellent Women* published by Jonathan Cape; Isabel Sutherland for the extract on p.27 from *Good Housekeeping; The Guardian* for the extract by Gail Kemp on p.28; *Cosmopolitan,* National Magazine Co. for the extract on p.30; William Heinemann Ltd for the extract on p.47 from *Dear Me* by Peter Ustinov, © Pavor SA, 1977; Marion Boyars Publishers Ltd for the extract on p.48 from *Medical Nemesis* by Ivan Illich; the *Western Mail* for the extract by G. Stoodly-Thomas on p.55; *The Guardian* for the extract on p.68; the Open University Press for the extract on p.69 from *Preparing to Study* by M.E. Richardson; George Weidenfeld and Nicolson Ltd for the extract on p.77 from *The Siege of Krishnapur* by John G. Farrell; *The Observer* for the extracts on p.91; Camera Press Ltd for the photograph on p.106; Barnabys Picture Library for the photographs on pp.108, 112 and 115; Sally and Richard Greenhill for the photograph on p.110; The Royal Ordnance for the advertisement on p.107; Oxfam for the advertisement on p.109; Yale University Press for the advertisement on p.113; the Youth Hostels Association for the advertisement on p.116; Longman Group UK Ltd for the cover illustration on p.117 from *Silas Marner* by George Eliot (Longman Study Texts); Penguin Books for the cover illustration on p.118 from *The Millstone* by Margaret Drabble.